THE HUMAN RIGHTS HANDBOOK

The Human Rights Handbook

a global perspective for education

Liam Gearon

Trentham Books
Stoke on Trent, UK and Sterling USA

Trentham Books Limited

Westview House	22883 Quicksilver Drive
734 London Road	Sterling
Oakhill	VA 20166-2012
Stoke on Trent	USA
Staffordshire	
England ST4 5NP	

2003 © Liam Gearon

First published 2003

British Library Cataloguing-in-Publication Data
A catalogue record for this book is available from the British Library

ISBN 1 85856 267 8

Typeset by Gabrielle, Chester and
printed in Great Britain by Cromwell Press Ltd., Wiltshire.

Contents

Introduction

The Human Rights Handbook: a global perspective for education is a practical text for teachers, students and researchers with a minimal background in the field of human rights. It does not claim to be comprehensive guide to all aspects of human rights but is designed to present an increasingly complex field in a simplified and accessible manner. This is important for several reasons. First, human rights are to do with individual and collective freedoms and responsibilities and, because of their universality, deserve to be better known at a more general level than they are at present. Human rights are not simply the province of lawyers and the legal professions. They affect all our lives.

Second, specifically in an educational context in the United Kingdom, and internationally, rights are increasingly features of compulsory curricula, in England through Citizenship (Osler, 2000, Gearon, 2003). Educators from all subject backgrounds at both primary and secondary level will find that rights permeate, and have the potential to enrich, all aspects of teaching and learning. The United Nations has consistently placed educators as the single most important agents for developing a truly global human rights culture.

Third, human rights provide a social justice perspective – *responsibilities* as well as *rights* – relevant to all aspects of human development: civil and political, economic, social and cultural life. Human rights discourse provides a uniquely international, collaborative and consensual framework for contributing to critically engaged education. That supposedly 'universal' rights (to equality of opportunity, to health, education, employment) are hardly universally distributed is more reason why understanding international standards is important.

How You Might Use This Handbook

The book is in three main sections. Part I – chapter 1 – provides a general overview of human rights in modern times. It provides a framework for understanding rights as international standards set by the United Nations but implemented on the ground in regional-governmental context and by the significant number of non-government organisations (NGOs) that deal with human rights and related issues.

Part II – chapters 2–11 – provides more detail on the central themes of human rights. This is the largest, substantive part of the book:

II.I

Civil and Political Rights

2. Genocide
3. Torture
4. Asylum
5. Slavery

II.II
Economic, Social and Cultural Rights

6. The Right to Development
7. Freedom of Expression and Censorship
8. Freedom of Religion and Belief

II.III
Human Solidarity

9. Children's Rights
10. Women's Rights
11. The Rights of Indigenous Peoples

The subdivisions of Part II – 'Civil and Political Rights', 'Economic, Social and Cultural Rights' and 'Human Solidarity' – recognises evolutionary refinements in human rights discourse, sometimes described as a three-generation model of rights (Wellman, 2000). Evidence of first generation rights, for example, can be found in the legal constitutions of England, France and America, and are often referred to as 'first-generation' rights. 'Second-generation' rights are built on the latter but address a wider range of social, cultural and economic rights. 'Third-generation' rights, while inherent in both first- and second- generation rights, are part of a recognition that certain groups in certain states have either suffered consistent historical injustice – indigenous peoples, for instance – or require special protection because of their inherently or potentially weaker status within society – for instance, children. These rights are discussed in Part III and, although they are relatively recent developments, are among the most vociferously fought for and defended.

Part III – chapter 12 – concerns the challenge of human rights education, especially in the promotion of knowledge, understanding and application of human rights. The term human rights education refers to education and educators in the widest sense. Human rights education crucially will take place in primary and secondary schools but it will also be a focus for education, training and research in colleges and universities as well as a range of other public sector bodies, from health to security.

The volume is designed with optimal accessibility in mind, each of the twelve chapters adopting the same format:

- **Chapter Headings** – summary of the treatment of a particular human right
- **Background Notes** – defining the human right in question
- **International Legal Standards** – how the human right in question is defended
- **Featured Document** – an extended summary of one key legal standard
- **Human Rights Organisations: UN, Regional-Governmental and NGO** – examples of bodies that deal with the human right in question
- **References, Further Reading and Research** – selected additional resources allow for greater study

References

Gearon, Liam (ed) (2003) *Learning to Teach Citizenship in the Secondary School* (London: Routledge)

Osler, Audrey (2000) *Citizenship and Democracy in Schools: Diversity, Identity, Equality* (Stoke on Trent: TrenthamBooks)

Wellman, Carl (2000) *The Proliferation of Rights: Moral Progress or Empty Rhetoric?* (Oxford: Westview)

I

Human Rights in Global Context

CHAPTER ONE

Universal Human Rights?

Background Notes

Figure 1.1

Universal Human Rights? Chapter Headings

In the aftermath of the First World War, the international community established the League of Nations to curtail some of the worst excesses of mass slaughter. That the League of Nations was powerless to prevent the genocide and slaughter on a genuinely global scale during the Second World War did not deter the international community from starting again after that war with the construction of another, not dissimilar organisation. Thus, the United Nations (UN) was born with grand aims of world peace and freedom in a tolerant world that worked by consensus but respected the diversity of cultures. The Charter of the UN (see Figure 1.2) was signed in 1945 in a world seemingly weary of war.

Figure 1.2

The Charter of the United Nations

The Charter of the United Nations was signed on 26 June 1945, in San Francisco, at the conclusion of the United Nations Conference on International Organisation, and came into force on 24 October 1945.

PREAMBLE

WE THE PEOPLES OF THE UNITED NATION DETERMINED
* to save succeeding generations from the scourge of war, which twice in our lifetime has brought untold sorrow to mankind, and

3

- to reaffirm faith in fundamental human rights, in the dignity and worth of the human person, in the equal rights of men and women and of nations large and small, and
- to establish conditions under which justice and respect for the obligations arising from treaties and other sources of international law can be maintained, and
- to promote social progress and better standards of life in larger freedom

AND FOR THESE ENDS
- to practice tolerance and live together in peace with one another as good neighbours, and
- to unite our strength to maintain international peace and security, and
- to ensure, by the acceptance of principles, and the institution of methods, that armed force shall not be used, save in the common interest, and
- to employ international machinery for the promotion of the economic and social advancement of all peoples,

HAVE RESOLVED TO COMBINE OUR EFFORTS TO ACCOMPLISH THESE AIMS.

Accordingly, our respective Governments, through representatives assembled in the city of San Francisco, who have exhibited their full powers found to be in good and due form, have agreed to the present Charter of the United Nations and do hereby establish an international organisation to be known as the United Nations.

CHAPTER I deals with **PURPOSES AND PRINCIPLES**, thus Article I states,
'The purposes of the United Nations are:

1. To maintain international peace and security, and to that end: to take effective collective measures for the prevention and removal of threats to the peace, and for the suppression of acts of aggression or other breaches of the peace, and to bring about by peaceful means, and in conformity with the principles of justice and international law, adjustment or settlement of international disputes or situations which might lead to a breach of the peace
2. To develop friendly relations among nations based on respect for the principle of equal rights and self-determination of peoples, and to take other appropriate measures to strengthen universal peace
3. To achieve international-operation in solving international problems of an economic, social, cultural, or humanitarian character, and in promoting and encouraging respect for human rights and fundamental freedoms for all without distinction as to race, sex, language, or religion, and
4. To be a centre for harmonizing the actions of nations in the attainment of these common ends.'

CHAPTER II deals with **MEMBERSHIP** of the United Nations.
Thus Article 4 states that 'Membership in the United Nations is open to all peace-loving states which accept the obligations contained in the present Charter and, in the judgment of the Organisation, are able and willing to carry out these obligations.'

CHAPTER III deals with **ORGANS** of the United Nations.
Thus, **Article 7** states that

1. 'There are established as the principal organs of the United Nations:

General Assembly
Security Council
Economic and Social Council
Trusteeship Council
International Court of Justice
A Secretariat

2. Such subsidiary organs as may be found necessary may be established in accordance with the present Charter.'

For a full text of the Charter, follow links at **www.un.org**

The century, though, was less than halfway over and there were to be more bloody regional conflicts, many based on religious and ethnic differences. It was too age of nuclear proliferation, especially evident during the height of the Cold War, when the world was threatened with the prospect of a Third, and nuclear, war. Weapons of mass destruction still abound, and many so-called rogue states still aim to develop them. Post-September 11, the war on terror has yet to abate. There is a clear discrepancy between the stated ideals and historical reality when it comes to the standards of the international community, as many histories of the UN show (Ryan, 2000). This book will highlight the successes as well as these manifold failings in relation to human rights. The distance between expressed aims for individual human beings and for international relations between nation-states remains perhaps the greatest and most pressing issue for human rights.

This discrepancy – between moral ideal and historical/political reality – was as evident at the time of the UN Charter as it is now, perhaps more so. The timing, for example, of the first signatures on the Charter on 26 June 1945 is chilling. These signatures appeared – with their commitment to peace amongst nations – less than two months before the dropping of the atom bombs on Hiroshima (August 6, 1945) and Nagazaki (August 8, 1945). At this time too, many of the European, world-wide, empires – of Britain and France, especially in Africa and Asia – were, if in imminent decline, nonetheless still in existence.

Figure 1.3 presents a simple timeline of the UN since its inception. It shows how the UN has developed exponentially into a truly global and far reaching organisation and how the UN Universal Declaration of Human Rights (1948), signed three years after the Charter, has proliferated into a complex of other declarations, covenants, conventions and world conferences.

Figure 1.3

Timeline

1940s
26 June 1945
Signing of the Charter of the United Nations (San Francisco, USA)
9 December 1945
Convention on the Prevention and Punishment of the Crime of Genocide
10 December 1945
Universal Declaration of Human Rights

1950s
4 November 1950
European Convention on Human Rights (Council of Europe)
28 July 1951
Convention relating to the Status of Refugees
20 December 1952
Convention on the Political Rights of Women
23 October 1953
Protocol amending the Slavery Convention (originally signed in Geneva, Switzerland, 25 September 1926
28 September 1954
Convention relating to the Status of Stateless Persons
7 September 1956
Convention on the Abolition of Slavery, the Slave Trade, and Institutions and Practices Similar to Slavery
25 June 1957
Convention on the Abolition of Forced Labour
20 November 1959
Declaration of the Rights of the Child

1960s
14 December 1960
Declaration on the Granting of Independence to Colonial Countries and Peoples
20 November 1963
Declaration on the Elimination of All Forms of Racial Discrimination
21 December 1965
International Convention on the Elimination of All Forms of Racial Discrimination
– Committee on the Elimination of All Forms of Racial Discrimination established
16 December 1966
International Covenant on Civil and Political Rights
International Covenant on Economic, Social and Cultural Rights
– Human Rights Committee established
7 November 1967
Declaration on the Elimination of Discrimination against Women
Proclamation of Teheran – International Conference on Human Rights
26 November 1968
Convention on the Non-Applicability of Statutory Limitations to War Crimes Against Humanity

1970s
30 November 1973
International Convention on the Suppression and Punishment of the Crime of Apartheid
9 December 1975
Declaration on the Protection of All Persons from being Subjected to Torture and Other Cruel, Inhuman or Degrading Treatment or Punishment

18 December 1979

Convention on the Elimination of All Forms of Discrimination against Women

– Committee on the Elimination of All Forms of Discrimination against Women established thereby

1980s

27 June 1981

African Charter on Human and Peoples' Rights (Organisation of African Unity)

25 November 1981

Declaration on the Elimination of All Forms of Intolerance and of Discrimination Based on Religion or Belief

10 December 1984

Convention against Torture and Other Cruel, Inhuman or Degrading Treatment or Punishment

28 May 1985

Committee on Economic, Social and Cultural Rights established to monitor implementation of International Covenant on Economic, Social and Cultural Rights.

4 December 1986

Declaration on the Right to Development

20 November 1989

Convention on the Rights of the Child

– Committee on the Rights of the Child established

15 December 1989

Second Optional Protocol to the International Covenant on Civil and Political Rights – aimed at the abolition of the death penalty

1990s

14 December 1990

Basic Principles for the Treatment of Principles

18 December 1990

International Convention on the Protection of the Rights of All Migrant Workers and members of their Families

18 December 1992

Declaration on the Protection of All Persons from Enforced Disappearance

Declaration on the Rights of Persons Belonging to National or Ethnic, Religious or Linguistic Minorities

14 June 1993

World Conference on Human Rights (Vienna) opens

25 June 1993

Vienna Declaration and Plan of Action

20 December 1993

Declaration on the Elimination of Violence against Women

Third Decade to Combat Racism and Racial Discrimination proclaimed (1995–2004)

Post of United Nations High Commissioner for Human Rights established

21 December 1993
International Decade of the World's Indigenous Peoples proclaimed
23 December 1994
United Nations Decade for Human Rights Education proclaimed (1995–2004)
1995
World Conference on Women's Rights (Beijing)
10 December 1998
Fiftieth Anniversary of the Universal Declaration of Human Rights

2000–
4–8 September 2001
World Conference against Racism, Xenophobia and All Forms of Discrimination (Durban, South Africa)

Further details at **www.un.org**

International Legal Standards

Human rights in the UN system imply universality. Yet human values are by their nature contested and history reveals a tragically imperfect world where inequalities abound and justice is too often absent.

On 10 September 2001, the New York-based Human Rights Watch reported on the United Nations' World Conference on Racism, Xenophobia and Related forms of Discrimination that had just ended in South Africa, a country once divided by State-sanctioned apartheid. Tensions had been evident between various factions for the brief duration of the conference. There was not full agreement on the proposal from Arab representatives that Zionism should be regarded as a form of racism. There was no consensus on the vexed question of reparation, especially by those presently rich, industrialized nations that had profited economically from the historical injustices of slavery. Yet there was seemingly broad agreement on the idea that discrimination on grounds of race, gender, culture and religion was an infringement of a moral universal right. If all could not agree fully on how to compensate for the evils of the past nor agree on how to resolve present difficulties, this United Nations conference ended by at least giving an impression that disparate countries and cultures were in agreement about broad principles, ethical universals now commonly categorized as human rights. The headline of the Human Rights Watch press release on 10 September read: 'Anti-Racism Summit Ends on Hopeful Note' (HRW, 2001). Twenty-four hours later, the world seemed a different place, almost a different planet (Gearon, 2002).

Yet September 11, while horrific, risks overstatement as a unique challenge to universal acceptance of international legal standards. A UN statement, for example, at the World Conference on Human Rights in Vienna (1993) expressed 'its dismay and condemnation that gross and systematic violations and situations that constitute serious obstacles to the full enjoyment of all human rights continue to occur in different parts of the world'. It continues:

> Such violations and obstacles include, as well as torture and cruel, inhuman and degrading treatment or punishment, summary and arbitrary executions, disappearances, arbitrary detentions, all forms of racism, racial discrimination and apartheid, foreign occupation and alien domination, xenophobia,

poverty, hunger and other denials of economic, social and cultural rights, religious intolerance, terrorism, discrimination against women and lack of the rule of law. (UN, 1993)

The 1993 World Conference on Human Rights resulted in the Vienna Plan of Action. This listed priorities for the global implementation of human rights. Five years after the World Conference on Human Rights, the United Nations Commissioner for Human Rights somewhat gloomily reported in his 1998 review of progress since Vienna:

> The international community must conclude that five years after Vienna, a wide gap continues to exist between the promise of human rights and their reality in the lives of people throughout the world. At the beginning of the twenty-first century, making all human rights a reality for all remains not only our fundamental challenge but our solemn responsibility. (UN, 1998)

It is this most fundamental sense of inequality that arguably presents the greatest challenge for teachers of citizenship and religious education, a disparity that is invariably the cause of conflict the world over. As Albert Camus (1948) once remarked, 'The spirit of revolt can only exist where a theoretic equality conceals great factual inequalities.' Few politicians and commentators can deny that the events and aftermath of 11 September are symptomatic of a wider historical struggle over values, a so-called clash of civilisations (Huntington, 1992), a clash made more apparent in the post cold-World War period (Haynes, 2000).

There are a number of related and equally contentious aspects to human rights in the context of this history. Economically and politically powerful countries, working for their own interests and those of their citizens, can make universal implementation difficult. Mansell (1999) highlights some of the most abused aspects of human rights discourse areas since the 1948 UN Universal Declaration of Human Rights:

> A study of the discourse of human rights since the Second World War suggests that the rhetoric of human rights has been determined most clearly by the propaganda value it represented:
>
> • The difference in the sort of human rights different states proclaimed was dictated by the political ideology of each state.
> • International institutions with power tend to reflect the interests of powerful states.
> • International financial institutions have, by their operation, made the protection of economic rights almost impossible for poor states.
> • The economic interests of wealthy states have led indirectly but regularly to human rights abuse whether, for instance, through the export of tobacco, the export of pesticides or the export of subsidised food.
> • The aftermath of colonialism continues to bedevil colonial peoples in their attempts to promote and secure self-determination.
> • Finally, regardless of proclaimed international standards on human rights, there are some states which may regularly, persistently and blatantly ignore world opinion if their strategic or emotional importance is exceptional. (Mansell, 1999)

The rest of this volume outlines and briefly assesses key themes in human rights – positive developments as well as contentious issues that arise from this history.

International legal standards are a modern phenomenon. Human rights documents and the legal standards contained therein divide into three basic forms:

Declarations
> – statements of good-intent by the UN General Assembly that are not strictly legally binding

Covenants
> – statements of a stronger level of guidance by the UN General Assembly but which are non-legally binding pledges and, if agreed by government representatives, are indications that a nation state will adhere to the particular human rights principles, and

Conventions
> – the strongest level of UN legal standard which if signed by governments become legally binding agreements by nation-states to adhere strictly to the guidance set out.

Conventions require a varying number of signatures from representatives of nation-states in order to be ratified and come into force.

Conventions also set out precisely how the terms of the agreement are to be managed, such as committee structure, composition, procedures for election and terms of reference, and so forth. (This is why conventions are always longer documents than basic statements of principle like Declarations.) Still, the supposed legal force of a convention hardly guarantees their implementation. If we take children's rights, for example, the most signed of all conventions is the 1989 Convention on the Rights of the Child. There are still, however, considerable concerns globally over the implementation of both spirit and letter of the convention – but the fact that a government like the United States (along with war-torn Somalia) has *not* signed such a convention does not mean that the US is in constant and blatant contravention of either the spirit or letter of the law. There are countries, by contrast, that have signed the Convention – one that constantly makes use of child soldiers, for instance – and are in breach of the spirit and the letter. Such discrepancies apply across all supposed international legal standards.

The Charter of the United Nations sets out the basic principles of goodwill and cooperation as a basis of principle on which international legal standards have developed in the 'UN era'. The basic international human rights are the International Bill of Human Rights. This International Bill of Human Rights is really *five* documents consisting of:

- Universal Declaration of Human Rights (10 December 1948)
- International Covenant on Economic, Social and Cultural Rights (16 December 1966, into effect 3 January 1976)
- International Covenant on Civil and Political Rights (16 December 1966, into effect 23 March 1976)
- Optional Protocol to the International Covenant on Civil and Political Rights (16 December 1966, into effect 23 March 1976)
- Second Optional Protocol to the International Covenant on Civil and Political Rights, aiming at the abolition of the death penalty (15 December 1989).

For the text and context of all these and the Charter, follow links on the website of the UN High Commissioner for Human Rights (UNHCHR) at **www.unhchr.org** or links through the UN homepage at **www.un.org**.

Featured Document: UN Universal Declaration of Human Rights

On December 10, 1948, the General Assembly of the United Nations adopted and proclaimed the Universal Declaration of Human Rights, the abbreviated text of which appears in the following pages. Following this historic act the Assembly called upon all Member countries to publicize the text of the Declaration and 'to cause it to be *disseminated, displayed, read and expounded principally in schools and other educational institutions*, without distinction based on the political status of countries or territories' (emphasis added).

All UN human rights documents – declarations, covenants and conventions – provide in legalistic and idealist language, often long and drawn-out, preambles of historical and moral context. The Preamble to UN Universal Declaration of Human Rights is no different, but it provides a foundation for modern-day human rights, worth citing in full:

> Whereas recognition of the inherent dignity and of the equal and inalienable rights of all members of the human family is the foundation of freedom, justice and peace in the world,
>
> Whereas disregard and contempt for human rights have resulted in barbarous acts which have outraged the conscience of mankind, and the advent of a world in which human beings shall enjoy freedom of speech and belief and freedom from fear and want has been proclaimed as the highest aspiration of the common people,
>
> Whereas it is essential, if man is not to be compelled to have recourse, as a last resort, to rebellion against tyranny and oppression, that human rights should be protected by the rule of law,
>
> Whereas it is essential to promote the development of friendly relations between nations,
>
> Whereas the peoples of the United Nations have in the Charter reaffirmed their faith in fundamental human rights, in the dignity and worth of the human person and in the equal rights of men and women and have determined to promote social progress and better standards of life in larger freedom,
>
> Whereas Member States have pledged themselves to achieve, in co-operation with the United Nations, the promotion of universal respect for and observance of human rights and fundamental freedoms,
>
> Whereas a common understanding of these rights and freedoms is of the greatest importance for the full realisation of this pledge,
>
> Now, therefore THE GENERAL ASSEMBLY proclaims THIS UNIVERSAL DECLARATION OF HUMAN RIGHTS as a common standard of achievement for all peoples and all nations, to the end that every individual and every organ of society, keeping this Declaration constantly in mind, shall strive by teaching and education to promote respect for these rights and freedoms and by progressive measures, national and international, to secure their universal and effective recognition and observance, both among the peoples of Member States themselves and among the peoples of territories under their jurisdiction. (UN, 1948)

It is a bold and forthright statement. Cynical observers have pointed out that the thinking is high on ideals but thin on processes that led to and underlie such wide-ranging anthropological, ethical, philosophical and political thinking (Forsythe, 2000).

But if this identifies a weakness in the especially the early UN documents, this feature also highlights something in their pragmatic nature. UN declarations and conventions are essentially political documents. Since the UN is at least in essence committed to the principles of democratic process – due representation of views and formal accounting of the acceptability through a voting consensus – such things take time. The democratic processes of discussion, voting and vast committee organisation needed for this to happen – we are talking about the General Assembly and vast global committees – means that the short statements that appear as final resolutions often reflect long periods of discussion, conflict before final resolution.

Indirectly, this means that different countries and cultures will input their own concerns before final resolution.

The UN today is far more representative than it was in 1948, with more than three times the number of nation-states represented at the UN General Assembly. Ironically, the 1948 Universal Declaration is certainly the least democratically representative of all UN documents in human rights though remaining the most foundational. (The irony that two key signatories, Britain and France, retained at the time of the UN Declaration exploitative vestiges of colonial empires in their overseas territories and dominions – is not lost on many developing nations.) In general, this is why there are ongoing debates about whether the original 30 articles have universal status as an outline statement of moral intent, let alone as a system of detailed ethical guidance (Gearon 2002).

Figure 1.4

UN Universal Declaration of Human Rights

Article 1
All human beings are born free and equal in dignity and rights.

Article 2
Everyone is entitled to all the rights and freedoms set forth in this Declaration, without distinction of any kind, such as race, colour, sex, language, religion, political or other opinion, national or social origin, property, birth or other status.

Article 3
Everyone has the right to life, liberty and security of person.

Article 4
No one shall be held in slavery or servitude; slavery and the slave trade shall be prohibited in all their forms.

Article 5
No one shall be subjected to torture or to cruel, inhuman or degrading treatment or punishment.

Article 6
Everyone has the right to recognition everywhere as a person before the law.

Article 7
All are equal before the law and are entitled without any discrimination to equal protection of the law.

Article 8
Everyone has the right to an effective remedy by the competent national tribunals for acts violating the fundamental rights.

Article 9
No one shall be subjected to arbitrary arrest, detention or exile.

Article 10

Everyone is entitled in full equality to a fair and public hearing by an independent and impartial tribunal.

Article 11

Everyone charged with a penal offence has the right to be presumed innocent until proved guilty according to law in a public trial.

Article 12

No one shall be subjected to arbitrary interference with privacy, family, home or correspondence.

Article 13

Everyone has the right to freedom of movement and residence within the borders of each state.

Article 14

Everyone has the right to seek and to enjoy in other countries asylum from persecution.

Article 15

Everyone has the right to a nationality.

Article 16

Men and women of full age, without any limitation due to race, nationality or religion, have the right to marry and to found a family.

Article 17

Everyone has the right to own property alone as well as in association with others.

Article 18

Everyone has the right to freedom of thought, conscience and religion.

Article 19

Everyone has the right to freedom of opinion and expression

Article 20

Everyone has the right to freedom of peaceful assembly and association.

Article 21

Everyone has the right to take part in the government of his country

Article 22

Everyone, as a member of society, has the right to social security.

Article 23

Everyone has the right to work.

Article 24

Everyone has the right to rest and leisure.

Article 25

Everyone has the right to a standard of living adequate for health and well-being.

Article 26

Everyone has the right to education.

Article 27

Everyone has the right freely to participate in the cultural life of the community.

Article 28

Everyone is entitled to a social and international order in which the rights and freedoms set forth in this Declaration can be fully realized.

Article 29

Everyone has duties to the community in which alone the free and full development of their personality is possible.

Article 30

Nothing in this Declaration may be interpreted as implying for any State, group or person any right to engage in any activity or to perform any act aimed at the destruction of any of the rights and freedoms set forth herein.

See **www.un.org** and follow link for the Universal Declaration, available in 300 languages. See also related link at **www.unhchr.org** and to human rights education in particular where a range of teaching and learning resources are available. See also, Amnesty International' site at **www.ai.org.uk**.

Given how wide-ranging the statement of human rights is – from basic civil and democratic political freedoms to rights of education, employment, health – it is not surprising that in an effort to make social progress through subsequent human rights work, the nature and extent of the rights framework has become extremely complex, not to say controversial.

Human Rights Organisations: UN, Regional-Governmental and NGO

The United Nations has developed considerably since its foundation in 1945. So too have the structures for its maintenance and the nature and complexity of human rights. The idea of three generations of human rights is worth restating from the introduction: civil and political, or first-generation rights; economic, social and cultural, or second-generation rights; and human solidarity, or third-generation rights. This crude measure recognises that rights have evolved in modern times by a series of historical-social-political developments. Foundational human rights documents in modern times were often the basis of new political constitutions. Legal rights set out in the Magna Carta, or in the English Bill of Rights, or rights set at the time of the French revolution are in this category, so are statements such as Thomas Pain's Declaration of the Rights of Man – which had such an influence on the American Constitution. The latter are called first generation rights because of this pre-UN context. The UN opened the way to developments on economic, social and cultural fronts that were less developed in these early English, French or American contexts. The 'latest generation' of human solidarity rights – relating to groups of individuals within a society such as women, children, minorities or indigenous peoples – would have been refinements in thinking largely inconceivable to the writers of 'first generation' civil, political and legal rights. (The best overview and critique of this proliferation of rights is by Wellman (2000) who asks whether such proliferation – the three generations of rights – can be regarded as moral progress of simply empty rhetoric.)

The development, then, of such new generations of universal human rights has been an integral feature of the development of the UN itself. It is difficult in modern times to separate the two: the development of universal human rights and the development of the United Nations are for better or worse entwined. This section is to highlight the organisations essential to the maintenance of the UN system of human rights. Three organisational levels are identifiable:

- The UN itself
- Regional-governmental bodies of the UN, nation states or supra-national governing structure (such as the European Community)
- Non-government organisations (NGOs).

Without at least one of these strands, successful implementation of human rights policy is unlikely.

1. The UN and Human Rights

The UN has its headquarters in New York and another major operating centre in Geneva, Switzerland. (These locations in wealthy nations are often cited as reasons why developing nations, especially, consider the UN has a western bias.) Home pages are at the following Internet address:

UN Headquarters – New York, USA
www.un.org

United Nations Office at Geneva (UNOG) – Geneva, Switzerland
www.unog.ch

The offices of the UN High Commissioner for Human Rights (**www.unhchr.ch**) – established since 1998 – is in Geneva. The appointment of a specially appointed UN Commissioner for Human Rights indicates the growing international importance of human rights in international politics.

The Secretary-General of the UN has therefore made human rights the central theme that 'unifies the organisation's work in the key areas of peace and security, development, humanitarian assistance and economic and social affairs'. Thus,

> Virtually every United Nations body and specialized agency is involved to some degree in the protection of human rights. One of the great achievements of the United Nations is the creation of a comprehensive body of human rights law, which, for the first time in history, provides us with a universal and internationally protected code of human rights, one to which all nations can subscribe and to which all people can aspire.

These include 'economic, social and cultural, as well as political and civil rights' and 'the established mechanisms with which to promote and protect these rights and to assist governments in carrying out their responsibilities' (UN, 2001). Figure 1.5 provides readers with an essential UN source for human rights research.

Figure 1.5

Further Research on the UN and Human Rights

United Nations Documentation: Research Guide

The United Nations is a major publisher. Over the more than five decades of its existence, it has published hundreds of thousands of documents (reports, studies, resolutions, meeting records, letters from Governments, etc.) on topics of key interest (disarmament, the environment, human rights, international law, peacekeeping, etc.).

Under the circumstances, it might initially seem impossible to track down precise information in view of the overwhelming amount of data available, but a systematic approach to your research will always yield results.

Given the vast number of UN documents and publications and the non-uniqueness or similarity of many titles – a nebulous request for the report of the Secretary-General, for example, will yield thousands of hits – it is helpful to pinpoint your research to a specific time-frame and, preferably, to limit it to a particular organ or subsidiary body. The beginner may be at a loss in this regard, but a number of basic reference tools are available to provide help.

The various editions of *Everyone's United Nations* concisely summarize major events in the Organisation's history. The researcher is given the forum (e.g., Security Council, General Assembly) before which and the year(s) during which the matter was discussed.

With these important pieces of information at hand, the next logical step might be to consult the *Yearbook of the United Nations* for the year(s) in question. The Yearbook will give a more detailed account, bibliographical citations to core documents available for consultation in depository libraries and UN Information Centres (or on the UN homepage for more recent years) and the full text of key resolutions.

For some researchers, the Yearbook may provide all the information required; others may prefer to exhaust the topic by going one level further: to the Index to Proceedings of the major organs (General Assembly, Security Council, Economic and Social Council, Trusteeship Council) to which the matter was presented. These highly specialized indexes are produced annually/sessionally and are comprehensive, including citations to every document relating to that organ's consideration of the topic.

The Encyclopedia of the United Nations also comes in handy for providing quick access to information of a general nature. Like the Yearbook, it very often cites the United Nations bodies involved and provides a time-frame, thereby enabling the reader to pinpoint his research more precisely should a more in-depth study be required.

The contents of *Basic Facts about the United Nations* are self-explanatory. This frequently updated handbook serves as a very handy, concise guide providing a condensed overview of United Nations activity in major spheres.

For more detailed research guidance to the UN system, visit the Dag Hammarskjöld Library, **www.un.org/Depts**

2. Regional-Governmental Human Rights

The work of the UN is supported by regional-governmental arrangements – nation states and regional offices of the UN itself. The importance of nation-states for upholding human rights was recognised by the 1993 World Conference on Human Rights at Vienna:

> The World Conference on Human Rights reaffirms the important and constructive role played by national institutions for the promotion and protection of human rights, in particular in their advisory capacity to the competent authorities, their role in remedying human rights violations, in the dissemination of human rights information, and education in human rights.The World Conference on Human Rights encourages the establishment and strengthening of national institutions, having regard to the 'Principles relating to the status of national institutions' and recognizing that it is the right of each State to choose the framework which is best suited to its particular needs at the national level. (UN, 1993: Para 36)

The second aspect of regional-governmental implementation relates to those organs of a particular UN body that oversee arrangements for UN policy at a trans-national and usually continental level, the importance of which was recognised by the 1993 World Conference on Human Rights at Vienna:

> Regional arrangements play a fundamental role in promoting and protecting human rights. They should reinforce universal human rights standards, as contained in international human rights instruments, and their protection. The World Conference on Human Rights endorses efforts under way to strengthen these arrangements and to increase their effectiveness, while at the same time stressing the importance of cooperation with the United Nations human rights activities. The World Conference on Human Rights reiterates the need to consider the possibility of establishing regional and sub-regional arrangements for the promotion and protection of human rights where they do not already exist. (UN, 1993: Para 37)

Examples of regional-governmental human rights organisations are represented in Figure 1.6.

Figure 1.6

Human Rights: Regional-Governmental Organisation

Africa
Economic Commission for Africa (ECA) – Addis Ababa, Ethiopia
www.uneca.org
Organisation of African Unity (OAU)
www.oau-oua.org

Americas and the Caribbean
Economic Commission for Latin America and the Caribbean (ECLAC) – Santiago, Chile
www.eclac.org
Organisation of American States (OAS)
www.oas.org
And related links to:
Inter-American Court of Human Rights
Inter-American Commission on Human Rights – IACHR
Inter-American Institute of Human Rights – IAIHR

Asia

Economic and Social Commission for Asia and the Pacific (ESCAP) – Bangkok, Thailand
www.unescap.org
Economic and Social Commission for Western Asia (ESCWA) – Beirut, Lebanon
www.escwa.org.lb

Europe

Economic Commission for Europe (ECE) – Geneva, Switzerland
www.unece.org
Council of Europe Directorate General of Human Rights
European Commission against Racism and Intolerance (ECRI)
www.ecri.coe.int
European Court of Human Rights
www.echr.coe.int

---

3. NGOs and Human Rights

NGOs play a crucial role in the promotion of every aspect of human rights. Many have representative status at the UN that means their views are solicited and listened to as part of UN policy-making. For a general statement of the relationship between the UN and the NGOs follow the links at **www.unog.ch**

At the Vienna World Conference on Human Rights the role of NGOs were regarded as essential to 'the promotion of all human rights and in humanitarian activities at national, regional and international levels':

> The World Conference on Human Rights appreciates their contribution to increasing public awareness of human rights issues, to the conduct of education, training and research in this field, and to the promotion and protection of all human rights and fundamental freedoms. While recognizing that the primary responsibility for standard-setting lies with States, the conference also appreciates the contribution of non-governmental organisations to this process. In this respect, the World Conference on Human Rights emphasizes the importance of continued dialogue and cooperation between Governments and non-governmental organisations. (UN, 1993: para 38)

The number of NGOs is immense and difficult to quantify exactly but would include charitable, aid, humanitarian and development organisations as well as those with the words 'human rights' in their titles (such as the New York-based Human Rights Watch). Figure 1.7 shows a representative range of NGOs across a number of continental regions.

Figure 1.7

NGOs across Continents

Africa

African Centre for the Constructive Resolution of Disputes (ACCORD)
www.accord.org.za
African Institute for Human Rights and Development
www.africaninstitute.org

Afronet
afronet.org.za/afronet
Southern African Human Rights NGO Network (SAHRINGON)
www.afronet.org.za/sahringon

Americas and Asia-Pacific
Asian Human Rights Commission (AHRC)
www.ahrchk.net
Asia-Pacific Forum on National Human Rights Institutions
www.apf.hreoc.gov.au
Asia Pacific Centre for Human Rights and the Prevention of Ethnic Conflict
wwwlaw.murdoch.edu.au/apchr
Directory of Organisations for Conflict Prevention in Asia and the Pacific
www.conflict-prevention.org
Human Rights in Latin America – LANIC
South Asia Human Rights Documentation Centre (SAHRDC)
www.hri.ca/partners/sahrdc
Lanic.utexas.edu/la/region/hrights
www.hrla.net
Human Rights Resource Center
www.hrusa.org

Europe
University of Essex Centre for Human Rights (University of Essex)
www.essex.ac.uk/chr
Centre for Research in Human Rights, University of Surrey Roehampton (CRHR)
www.roehampton.ac.uk/crhr
Consortium of Minority Resources (COMIR)
www.lgi.osi.hu/comir
European Centre for Minority Issues (ECMI)
www.ecmi.de
European Platform for Conflict Prevention and Transformation
www.euconflict.org
European Roma Rights Center (ERRC)
www.errc.org
Federal Union of European Nationalities (FUEN)
www.fuen.org
International Helsinki Federation for Human Rights (IHF)
www.ihf-hr.org
Minority Electronic Resources (MINELRES)
www.riga.lv/minelres
Open Society Institute Budapest
www.osi.hu/colpi

Statewatch
www.statewatch.org

General link of UN and the NGOs
www.unog.ch/

References, Further Reading and Research

Camus, Albert (1948) *The Rebel* (Harmondsworth: Penguin)

Forsythe, David P. (2000) *Human Rights in International Relations* (Cambridge: Cambridge University Press)

Gearon, Liam (ed) (2002) *Human Rights and Religion: A Reader* (Brighton and Portland: Sussex Academic Press)

Haynes, Jeff (2000) 'Religion' in Brian White, Richard Little and Michael Smith (eds) *Issues in Global Politics*, second edition (Basingstoke: Palgrave)

HRW (2001) 'Anti-Racism Summit Ends on Hopeful Note' (New York: Human Rights Watch 2001)

Huntington, Samuel (1993) *The Clash of Civilisations* (Washington, D.C.: American Enterprise Institute)

Mansell, Wade (1999) in Bell (ed) *Teaching Human Rights* (Warwick: Warwick Legal Centre)

Ryan, Stephen *The United Nations and International Politics* (London: Macmillan, 2000)

Sellar, Kirsten (2002) *The Rise and Rise of Human Rights* (London Sutton)

UN (1993) *The Vienna Declaration* (New York: UN)

UN (1998) Review of Vienna Statement by the United Nations High Commissioner for Human Rights (New York: United Nations)

UN (2001) Statement by Secretary-General of the United Nations (New York: United Nations)

UN (2002) *International Bill of Human Rights*, Fact Sheet 2 (New York: United Nations)

UN (2002) *Civil and Political Rights*, Fact Sheet 15 (New York: United Nations)

UN (2002) *National Institutions for the Promotion and Protection of Human Rights* (New York: United Nations)

UN (2002) *Seventeen frequently Asked Questions about United Nations Special Rapporteurs*, Fact Sheet 27 (New York: United Nations)

UN (2002) *United Nations Action in the Field of Human Rights* (New York: United Nations)

UN (2002) *United Nations Action in the Field of Human Rights* (New York: United Nations)

UN (2002) *Human Rights: A Compilation of International Instruments,* Vol 1, Parts I and II (New York: United Nations)

UN (2002) *Human Rights: A Compilation of International Instruments* – Regional Instruments, Vol II (New York: United Nations)

UN (2002) *Selected Decisions of the Human Rights Committee under the Optional Protocol* (New York: United Nations)

UN (1993) *World Conference on Human Rights: The Vienna Declaration and Programme of Action* (New York: United Nations)

Wellman, Carl *The Proliferation of Rights: Moral Progress or Empty Rhetoric?* (Oxford: Westview, 2000)

II

Defining and Defending Human Rights

I
Civil and Political Rights

CHAPTER TWO

Genocide

Everyone has the right to life, liberty and security of person.
Article 3, UN Universal Declaration of Human Rights

Figure 2.1

Genocide: Chapter Headings

Background Notes: Defining Genocide

International human rights are a modern phenomenon. They arise from a particular set of circumstances, namely, the ending of the Second World War. The world was confronted with the mechanisation of mass slaughter, human death on a truly industrial scale. While non-combatants have always been casualties in any armed conflicts, slaughter of civilian populations extended far beyond any previous scale. The industrialisation of death on a mass scale was also consciously directed at specific ethnic, cultural and religious elements of national populations. The Nazi Holocaust helped define our notions of genocide. And, though increasingly contentious as a term, it was genocide that was on the mind of the newly formed UN when considering a Universal Declaration of Human Rights, and when it finally made the Declaration in the form of 30 articles on 10 December 1948.

Yet it was the day before on 9 December 1948 that the UN made the Declaration on the Prevention of Genocide, indicating some sense of priority and the originating needs of such a

23

Universal Declaration. Arguably, genocide defines the subsequent contours of the UN mandate in the others areas of its operation, set to expand drastically over coming decades (Ryan, 2000). Arguably, it is the violence and horror of genocide that are foundational motivations behind all human rights legislation.

Genocide can be defined as the systematic elimination of a targeted population. It might be undertaken because of their ethnic or racial identity. One of the most deeply disturbing reflections of the World Conference on Human Rights (Vienna, 1993) must have been 'its dismay at massive violations of human rights' especially in the form of genocide, 'ethnic cleansing' and systematic rape of women in war situations, creating mass exodus of refugees and displaced persons. While strongly condemning such abhorrent practices it reiterates the call that 'perpetrators of such crimes be punished and such practices immediately stopped' (Para 28). It recalls the 'disregard of standards as contained in international human rights instruments and international humanitarian law and about the lack of sufficient and effective remedies for the victims' and was 'deeply concerned about violations of human rights during armed conflicts, affecting the civilian population, especially women, children, the elderly and the disabled' (Para 29).

These statements from 1993 came two years before the worst single genocidal incidence since the Holocaust, with the slaughter in Rwanda, in central Africa. More widely, a review of the statistics for mass slaughter (as in Figure 2.2) – whether we terms this genocide or ethnic cleansing – *since* the 1948 Convention on the Prevention of Genocide makes particularly depressing reading.

Figure 2.2

Date	State	Victims	Deaths
1943–1957	USSR	Chechens, Ingushi, Karachi	230,000
1944–68	USSR	Crimean Tartars, Meskhetians	57,000–175,000
1955–77	China	Tibetans	Not available
1959–75	Iraq	Kurds	Not available
196272	Paraguay	Ache Indians	90,000
1963–64	Rwanda	Tutsis	5,000–14,000
1963	Laos	Meo Tribesmen	18,000–20,000
1965–66	Indonesia	Chinese	500,000–1 million
1965–73	Burundi	Hutus	103,000–205,000
1966	Nigeria	Ibos in North	9,000–30,000
1966–84	Guatemala	Indians	30,000–63,000
1968–85	Philippines	Moros	10,000–100,000
	Equatorial Guinea	Bubi Tribe	1,000–50,000
1971	Pakistan	Bengalis of Eastern Pakistan	1.25–3 million
1971–9	Uganda	Karamajong	100,000–500,000
		Acholi, Lango	Not available

1975–79	Cambodia	Muslim Cham	Not available
1975–98	Indonesia	East Timorese	60,000–200,000
1978–	Burma	Muslims in border regions	Not available
1979–86	Uganda	Karamanjong, Nilotic Tribes Bagandans	50,000–100,000
1981	Iran	Kurds, Bahais	10,000–20,000
1983–7	Sri Lanka	Tamils	2,000–10,000
1994	Rwanda	Tutsis	500,000–1 million
	Bosnia-Herzegovina	Mainly Bosnian Muslims	200,000

(Ryan, 2000)

International Legal Standards: Defending against Genocide

Since genocide (including war crimes and crimes against humanity) is so fundamental to international human rights, the Charter of the UN and the International Bill of Human Rights provide a foundation for understanding those documents listed in Figure 2.3.

Figure 2.3

International Legal Standards: Defending against Genocide

Convention on the Prevention and Punishment of the Crime of Genocide (9 December 1948, into effect 12 January 1951)

Convention on the Non-Applicability of Statutory Limitations to War Crimes and Crimes against Humanity (29 November 1968, into effect 11 November 1970)

Principles of international co-operation in the detection, arrest, extradition and punishment of persons guilty of war crimes and crimes against humanity (3 December 1973)

For the texts of these all these documents, follow the links at
www.unhchr.ch

Given that crimes against humanity and genocide often happen in times of armed civil conflict and war, the international legal standards on humanitarian law listed in Figure 2.4 can also have a bearing upon both.

Figure 2.4

International Legal Standards

Humanitarian Law

Geneva Convention for the Amelioration of the Condition of the Wounded and Sick in Armed Forces in the Field (21 April–12 August 1949, into effect 21 October 1950)

Geneva Convention for the Amelioration of the Condition of Wounded, Sick and Ship-wrecked Members of Armed Forces at Sea (21 April–12 August 1949, into effect 21 October 1950)

Geneva Convention relative to the Treatment of Prisoners of War (21 April–12 August 1949, into effect 21 October 1950)

Geneva Convention relative to the Protection of Civilian Persons in Time of War (21 April–12 August 1949, into effect 21 October 1950)

Protocol Additional to the Geneva Conventions of 12 August 1949, and relating to the Protection of Victims of International Armed Conflicts (Protocol I) (8 June 1977, into effect 1979)

Protocol Additional to the Geneva Conventions of 12 August 1949, and relating to the Protection of Victims of Non-International Armed Conflicts (Protocol II) (8 June 1977, into effect 1979)

For the texts of these all these documents, follow the links at **www.unhchr.ch**

The Convention on the Prevention and Punishment of the Crime of Genocide, summarised in Figure 2.5, signed on 9 December 1948, was the day before the UN's General Assembly approval of the Universal Declaration of Human Rights.

Figure 2.5

Featured Document

Convention on the Prevention and Punishment of the Crime of Genocide
9 December 1948, entry into force 12 January 1951

The Preamble of the Convention contains the following rationale:
'Having considered the declaration made by the General Assembly of the United Nations . . . that genocide is a crime under international law, contrary to the spirit and aims of the United Nations and condemned by the civilized world', it recognizes that

'at all periods of history genocide has inflicted great losses on humanity', and that

'in order to liberate mankind from such an odious scourge, international co-operation is required'.

This statement is the basis of the 19 articles of the convention.

Article 1 states that 'Genocide, whether committed in time of peace or in time of war, is a crime under international law' which the international community undertakes to prevent and to punish.

Article 2 states that 'In the present Convention, genocide means any of the following acts committed with intent to destroy, in whole or in part, a national, ethnic, racial or religious group, as such:

(a)   Killing members of the group;

(b) Causing serious bodily or mental harm to members of the group;
(c) Deliberately inflicting on the group conditions of life calculated to bring about its physi-
     cal destruction in whole or in part;
(d) Imposing measures intended to prevent births within the group;
(e) Forcibly transferring children of the group to another group.'

Article 3 states that the following acts shall be punishable:

'(a) Genocide;
(b) Conspiracy to commit genocide;
(c) Direct and public incitement to commit genocide;
(d) Attempt to commit genocide;
(e) Complicity in genocide.'

Article 4 states that 'Persons committing genocide or any of the other acts enumerated in article 3 shall be punished, whether they are constitutionally responsible rulers, public officials or private individuals.'

Article 5 states that 'The Contracting Parties undertake to enact, in accordance with their respective Constitutions, the necessary legislation to give effect to the provisions of the present Convention, and, in particular, to provide effective penalties for persons guilty of genocide or any of the other acts enumerated [in article 3].'

Article 6 states that 'Persons charged with genocide . . . shall be tried by a competent tribunal of the State in the territory of which the act was committed, or by such international penal tribunal as may have jurisdiction with respect to those Contracting Parties which shall have accepted its jurisdiction.'

Article 7 states that 'Genocide and the other acts enumerated shall not be considered as political crimes for the purpose of extradition. The Contracting Parties pledge themselves in such cases to grant extradition in accordance with their laws and treaties in force.'

Article 8 states that 'Any Contracting Party may call upon the competent organs of the United Nations to take such action under the Charter of the United Nations as they con-sider appropriate for the prevention and suppression of acts of genocide or any of the other acts enumerated in article 3.'

Articles 9 to **19** concern disputes between contracting parties (**Article 9**), the translation of the document (**Article 10**), signing and ratification (**Article 11**), extending applicability of the convention to the foreign territories of the contracting parties (**Article 12**), means by which the Convention comes into force (**Article 13**), period of effectiveness of the con-vention (**Article 14**), denunciation (**Article 15**), processes for revision (**Article 16**), pro-cedures for notifying signatories to the Convention (**Article 17**), deposition of the original Convention in the UN archives (**Article 18**), registration of the Convention with the Secretary-General of the UN (**Article 19**).

For the full text, follow links at **www.unhchr.org**

Human Rights Organisations Concerned with Genocide: UN, Regional-Governmental and NGO

1. UN: The International Criminal Court

One of the major developments in human rights is the development of the International Criminal Court. Full details are on the UN International Criminal Court (ICC) site, **www.www.un.org.law/icc**. Figure 2.6, an ICC Fact Sheet adapted from Human Rights Watch (HRW) identifies frequently asked questions about the International Criminal Court.

Figure 2.6

The International Criminal Court

The International Criminal Court (ICC) is a permanent tribunal that will investigate and try individuals for the most serious international crimes: genocide, crimes against humanity, and war crimes. The ICC will be the first standing court of its kind, a unique and important development in the history of human rights protection and international justice. The court will only act in cases where states are unwilling or unable to do so – known as the principle of complementarity.

Who

The International Criminal Court will prosecute individuals – not states. The court will consist of eighteen elected judges and an elected prosecutor, who will lead investigations and try cases. Only those states who have ratified the treaty will be able to nominate and elect judges and prosecutors.

When

On July 17, 1998, one hundred and twenty countries voted to adopt the treaty outlining the establishment and structure of the International Criminal Court. Since then, 139 countries have signed the treaty and 71 countries have ratified it. The treaty "enters into force" on July 1, 2002 and the ICC can then begin its work. The court can only take cases that occur after this point. This means that crimes committed before this moment in time cannot be brought to the court – this is known as non-retroactivity.

Where

The International Criminal Court will be based in the Hague, the Netherlands. The ICC will have jurisdiction over crimes committed in the territories of ratifying states and over crimes committed anywhere by nationals of ratifying states. States that do not ratify the treaty can choose to accept the court's jurisdiction in particular cases. These states, and all states parties, must cooperate with the court's investigations and prosecutions.

Why

The International Criminal Court will bring the most serious international criminals to justice and challenge the impunity that they have so often enjoyed in the past. Until now, those who commit atrocities have gotten away with it and their victims left with nothing. The ICC can provide redress and reparations for the victims and survivors of these atrocities, which is a vital step towards accountability and lasting justice.

How

There are three ways that cases can be brought to the International Criminal Court. Both a state that has joined the treaty and the Security Council of the United Nations can refer a situation to the court for investigation. In addition, the ICC prosecutor can start an investigation based on information that she or he receives from victims, non-governmental organisations, or any other reliable source. The ICC will rely on state cooperation in its investigation and prosecution of cases. The ICC will not have its own police force and will work side by side with national authorities.

For the full text, visit **www.hrw.org**

Figure 2.7 provides a list of useful links related to the ICC.

Figure 2.7

ICC Links

UN International Criminal Court Site
http://www.un.org/law/icc

International Coalition for the ICC
http://www.igc.org/icc/html/coalition
Council of Europe page on the International Criminal Court
http://www.legal.coe.int/criminal/icc

Amnesty International ICC Site
http://www.amnesty.org.uk/action/camp/icc

Women's Caucus for Gender Justice
http://www.iccwomen.org/icc
International Criminal Court Internet Library
http://www.lib.uchicago.edu/~llou/icc.html#internet

---

2. *REGIONAL-GOVERNMENTAL: Organisation of African Unity*

The ferocity of ethnic violence between Hutu and Tutsi in Rwanda and neighbouring central African states took the world by surprise. It seemed powerless, or simply unwilling to intervene. Half a million African people, and perhaps more, lost their lives in months of genocidal violence in Rwanda during 1994. In Europe, the conflict in the Balkans and the full extent of the 'ethnic cleansing' there had yet to draw to a formal peacekeeping close. In Rwanda, all the world could do was to act after the carnage. In accordance with Chapter VII of the United Nations Charter – which held up such high ideals of peace, freedom, respect for human rights and the dignity of the person – the Security Council created the International Criminal Tribunal for Rwanda (ICTR) on 8 November 1994 to try any persons responsible for crimes against humanity over the full course of 1994. The purpose of this measure was 'to contribute to the process of national reconciliation in Rwanda and to the maintenance of peace in the region'. Early in 1995, the Security Council resolved that the Tribunal would be based in the United Republic of Tanzania. Figure 2.8 provides 'at a glance' the role, jurisdiction and basic composition of the Tribunal.

Figure 2.8

Genocide in Rwanda: The Tribunal at a Glance

Role and Jurisdiction

The International Criminal Tribunal for Rwanda (ICTR) was established by the Security Council of the United Nations to prosecute persons responsible for genocide and other serious violations of international humanitarian law committed in the territory of Rwanda between 1 January 1994 and 31 December 1994. It may also prosecute Rwandan citizens charged with such crimes committed in the territory of neighbouring states during the same period. The purpose of this measure was to contribute to the process of national reconciliation in Rwanda and to the maintenance of peace in the region, replacing an existing culture of impunity with one of accountability. Only with the commitment to justice of the international community can the architects of the Rwandan genocide, who have fled to countries around the world, be held legally accountable for their actions. Through the creation of the ICTR, the international community demonstrates that it will not tolerate crimes of genocide.

Chambers

The judges of the Tribunal are elected by the General Assembly of the United Nations. No two of them may be nationals of the same State. Three judges sit in each of the Trial Chambers and seven judges are members of the Appeals Chamber, which is shared with the International Criminal Tribunal for the former Yugoslavia and is based in the Hague, the Netherlands.

Enforcement of Sentences

Convicted persons will serve their sentences in countries that have made agreements with the ICTR to enforce such sentences. These countries will not have the authority to alter the terms of the incarceration without the consent of the ICTR. The Tribunal prefers that these sentences are served in Africa for socio-cultural reasons. Mali, the Republic of Benin and the Kingdom of Swaziland have signed such agreements.

Further details available at **www.ictr.org**

The Organisation of African Unity site (**www.oau.org**) includes the Report by the International Panel of Eminent Personalities to Investigate the 1994 Genocide in Rwanda and the Surrounding Events. It can be found by following links to Links to this and genocide in Europe in the same decade can be found in Figure 2.9.

Figure 2.9

Genocide and Ethnic Cleansing in Africa and Europe

International Criminal Tribunal for Rwanda
www.un.org/ictr
International Criminal Tribunal for the Former Yugoslavia
www.un.org/icty

The ICTR site has useful links to the following:

ICTR Library
United Nations sites
International Criminal Court
Other International Organisations
Research Institutes and Libraries
Media Links
Non-Governmental Organisations

Further details available at **www.ictr.org**

As figures for instances of post-1948 genocide demonstrate (see Figure 2.2), ethnicity continues to be an important element in such conflict. The United Nations Research Institute for Social Development (UNRISD), based in Geneva (**www.unrisd.org/**) has a number of research programmes directed at this area of conflict and conflict resolution, including the following research documents:

The Search for Identity Ethnicity Religion and Political Violence
www.unrisd.org/engindex/publ/list/op/op6/op06-03

Ethnic Violence Conflict Resolution and Cultural Pluralism
www.unrisd.org/engindex/publ/list/conf/eth1/eth1-04

Ethnic Diversity and Public Policy: An Overview
www.unrisd.org/engindex/publ/list/op/op8/op08-05

3. NGO: Beth Shalom

Beth Shalom is the UK's first museum dedicated to the commemoration of and education about the Holocaust. Founded and directed by Stephen Smith, Beth Shalom Web Centre contains three related sites:

Holocaustcentre.net – the nature and purpose of the Beth Shalom Holocaust Centre.

Holocausthistory.net – an introduction to the Holocaust in historical context.

Holocaustbookstore.net – an online retail store run by Beth Shalom, specialising exclusively in Holocaust and Genocide related books and resources.

Beth Shalom also oversees a number of research projects:

Aegistrust.org – Aegis Genocide Prevention Initiative to identify the causes, predict the development and prevent the incidence of genocide.

RFTF.org – Remembering for the Future is a scholarly and research-focused forum of genocide and Holocaust studies.

Figure 2.10 contains links to wider studies of genocide – for education, research and prevention.

Figure 2.10

Genocide NGO Links

International Crisis Group
www.crisisweb.org

FEWER
www.fewer.org

Genocide Watch
www.genocidewatch.org

International Alert
www.international-alert.org

The Organisation for Security and Co-operation in Europe (OSCE)
www.osce.org

Prevent Genocide International
www.preventgenocide.org

Saferworld
www.saferworld.co.uk

References, Further Reading and Research

Allen, Michael Thad (2002) *The Business of Genocide: The SS, Slave Labour and the Concentration Camps* (Chapel Hill, NC: University of North Carolina Press)

Ball, Howard (1999) *Prosecuting War Crimes and Genocide: The Twentieth-Century Experience* (Lawrence: University Press of Kansas)

Bartov, Omer and Phyllis Mack (eds) 2001 *In God's Name: Genocide and Religion in the Twentieth Century* (Oxford: Berghahn Books)

Chandler, David P. *Voices from S-21: Terror and History in Pol Pot's Secret Prison* (Berkeley: University of California Press)

Charny, Israel W. (ed) (1999) *Encyclopedia of Genocide*, forewords by Desmond M. Tutu and Simon Wiesenthal (Santa Barbara, California: ABC-CLIO)

Chorbajian, Levon and George Shirnian (eds) (1999) *Studies in Comparative Genocide* (Basingstoke: Macmillan)

Dadrian, Vahakn N. (1999) *Warrant for Genocide: Key Elements of Turko-Armenian Conflict* (New Brunswick, NJ: Transaction Publishers)

Department of Education and Employment (2000) *Holocaust Memorial Day: Remembering Genocides, Lessons for the Future Education Pack* (London: DfEE)

Gourevitch, Philip (1999) *We Wish to Inform You That Tomorrow We Will Be Killed With Our Families: Stories from Rwanda* (London: Picador)

Hinton, Alexander Laban (ed) (2002) *Genocide: An Anthropological Reader* (Malden: Blackwell Publishers)

Kressel, Neil J. *Mass Hate: The Global Rise of Genocide and Terror* (Cambridge, MA: Westview)

Lorey, David E. and William H. Beezley (eds) (2002) *Genocide, Collective Violence and Popular Memory: The Politics of Remembrance in the Twentieth Century* (Wilmington, Del: SR Books)

Rosenbaum, Alan S. (ed) (2001) *Is the Holocaust Unique?: Perspectives on Comparative Genocide* (Oxford: Westview Press)

Ryan, Stephen *The United Nations and International Politics* (London: Macmillan, 2000)

Schabas, William (2000) *Genocide in International Law: The Crime of Crimes* (Cambridge: Cambridge University Press)

Smith, Helmut Walser (ed) *The Holocaust and Other Genocides: History, Representation, Ethics* (Nashville: Vanderbilt University Press)

Supple, Carrie (1999) *From Prejudice to Genocide: Learning about the Holocaust* (Stoke on Trent: Trentham Books)

United Nations (2002) *Extrajudicial, Summary or Arbitrary Executions*, Fact Sheet 11 (New York: United Nations)

United Nations (2002) *The International Bill of Human Rights*, Fact Sheet 1 (New York: United Nations)

Waller, James (2002) *Becoming Evil: How Ordinary People Commit Genocide and Mass Killing* (Oxford: Oxford University Press)

Weine, Stevan M (1999) *When History is a Nightmare: Lives and Memories of Ethnic Cleansing in Bosnia-Herzogovina* (New Brunswick, NJ: Rutgers University Press)

CHAPTER THREE

Torture

Figure 3.1

Torture: Chapter Headings

Background Notes: Defining Torture

Article 1 of the Convention against Torture and Other Cruel, Inhuman or Degrading Treatment or Punishment (Adopted 10 December 1984) defines torture as:

> . . . any act by which severe pain or suffering, whether physical or mental, is intentionally inflicted on a person for such purposes as obtaining from him or a third person information or a confession, punishing him for an act he or a third person has committed or is suspected of having committed, or intimidating or coercing him or a third person, or for any reason based on discrimination of any kind, when such pain or suffering is inflicted by or at the instigation of or with the consent or acquiescence of a public official or other person acting in an official capacity.

This 'does not include pain or suffering arising only from, inherent in or incidental to lawful sanctions'. The Convention builds on the 1975 Declaration against Torture and Other Cruel, Inhuman or Degrading Treatment or Punishment. It accords with 'the principles proclaimed in the Charter of the United Nations, [that] recognition of the equal and inalienable rights of all members of the human family is the foundation of freedom, justice and peace in the world'. It intended 'to make more effective the struggle against torture and other cruel, inhuman or degrading treatment or punishment throughout the world'.

International Legal Standards: Defending against Torture

Two key areas where torture features in international legal standards are human rights in the administration of justice (especially in the treatment of prisoners) and humanitarian law (again, often likely to relate to prisoners, here of war). Figures 3.2 and 3.3 outline some of the major international standards that have a direct or indirect bearing on torture.

Figure 3.2

International Legal Standards: Defending against Torture

Human Rights in the Administration of Justice

Standard Minimum Rules for the Treatment of Prisoners (1955; 31 July 1957; 13 May 1977)

Code of Conduct for Law Enforcement Officials (17 December 1979)

Principles of Medical Ethics relevant to the Role of Health Personnel, particularly Physicians, in the Protection of Prisoners and Detainees against Torture and Other Cruel, Inhuman or Degrading Treatment or Punishment (18 December 1982)

Safeguards guaranteeing protection of the rights of those facing the death penalty ((25 May 1984)

Basic Principles on the Independence of the Judiciary (26 August–6 September 1985/29 November 1985/13 December 1985)

Declaration on the Protection of All Persons from Being Subjected to Torture and Other Cruel, Inhuman or Degrading Treatment or Punishment (10 December 1984, into effect 26 June 1987)

Body of Principles for the Protection of All Persons under Any Form of Detention or Imprisonment (9 December 1988)

Principles on the Effective Prevention and Investigation of Extra-legal, Arbitrary and Summary Executions (29 May 1989)

Declaration of Basic Principles of Justice for Victims of Crime and Abuse of Power (29 November 1985)
United Nations Standard Minimum Rules for the Administration of Juvenile Justice ('The Beijing Rules') (29 November 1989)

Basic Principles on the Use of Force and Firearms by Law Enforcement Officials (27 August– 7 October 1990)

Basic Principles on the Role of Lawyers (27 August–7 October 1990)

Guidelines on the Role of Prosecutors (27 August–7 October 1990)

United Nations Standard Minimum Rules for Non-custodial Measures ('The Tokyo Rules') (10 December 1990)

United Nations Rules for the Protection of Juveniles Deprived of their Liberty (14 December 1990)

Basic Principles for the Treatment of Prisoners (14 December 1990)

United Nations Guidelines for the Prevention of Juvenile Delinquency (The Riyadh Guidelines) (14 December 1990)

Model Treaty on the Transfer of Proceedings in Criminal Matters (14 December 1990)

Model Treaty on the Transfer of Supervision of Offenders Conditionally Sentenced or Conditionally Released (14 December 1990)

Declaration on the Protection of All Persons from Enforced Disappearances (18 December 1992)

Principles on the Effective Investigation and Documentation of Torture and Other Cruel, Inhuman or Degrading Treatment or Punishment (2 December 2000)

Convention against Torture and Other Cruel, Inhuman or Degrading Treatment or Punishment (4 December 2000)

For the texts of these all these documents, follow the links on **www.unhchr.ch**

Figure 3.3

International Legal Standards: Torture

Humanitarian Law

Geneva Convention for the Amelioration of the Condition of the Wounded and Sick in Armed Forces in the Field

Geneva Convention for the Amelioration of the Condition of the Wounded, Sick and Shipwrecked Members of Armed Forces at Sea

Geneva Convention relative to the Treatment of Prisoners of War

Geneva Convention relative to the Treatment of Civilians in Time of War

Protocol Additional to the Geneva Convention of 12 August 1949, and relating to the Protection of Victims of International Armed Conflicts (Protocol I)

Protocol Additional to the Geneva Convention of 12 August 1949, and relating to the Protection of Victims of International Armed Conflicts (Protocol II)

For the texts of these all these documents, follow the links on **www.unhchr.ch**

The foundational document, however, of which Figure 3.4 provides the main text, is the Declaration on the Protection of All Persons from Being Subjected to Torture and Other Cruel, Inhuman or Degrading Treatment or Punishment.

Figure 3.4

Featured Document

Declaration on the Protection of All Persons from Being Subjected to Torture and Other Cruel, Inhuman or Degrading Treatment or Punishment
9 December 1975

Article 1 defines, for the purpose of the Declaration, torture as 'any act by which severe pain or suffering, whether physical or mental, is intentionally inflicted by or at the instigation of a public official on a person for such purposes as obtaining from him or a third person information or confession, punishing him for an act he has committed or is suspected of having committed, or intimidating him or other persons'. This 'does not include pain or suffering arising only from, inherent in or incidental to, lawful sanctions to the extent consistent with the Standard Minimum Rules for the Treatment of Prisoners'. In other words, 'Torture constitutes an aggravated and deliberate form of cruel, inhuman or degrading treatment or punishment.'

Article 2 states that 'Any act of torture or other cruel, inhuman or degrading treatment or punishment is an offence to human dignity and shall be condemned as a denial of the purposes of the Charter of the United Nations and as a violation of the human rights and fundamental freedoms proclaimed in the Universal Declaration of Human Rights.'

Article 3 demands that 'No State may permit or tolerate torture or other cruel, inhuman or degrading treatment or punishment. Exceptional circumstances such as a state of war or a threat of war, internal political instability or any other public emergency may not be invoked as a justification of torture or other cruel, inhuman or degrading treatment or punishment.'

Article 4 gives responsibility for each State in accordance with the provisions of the Declaration to 'take effective measures to prevent torture and other cruel, inhuman or degrading treatment or punishment from being practised within its jurisdiction'.

Article 5 states that 'The training of law enforcement personnel and of other public officials who may be responsible for persons deprived of their liberty shall ensure that full account is taken of the prohibition against torture and other cruel, inhuman or degrading treatment or punishment. This prohibition shall also, where appropriate, be included in such general rules or instructions as are issued in regard to the duties and functions of anyone who may be involved in the custody or treatment of such persons.'

Article 6 commits each State to keeping 'under systematic review interrogation methods and practices as well as arrangements for the custody and treatment of persons deprived of their liberty in its territory, with a view to preventing any cases of torture or other cruel, inhuman or degrading treatment or punishment'.

Article 7 commits each State to ensuring 'that all acts of torture as defined in article 1 are offences under its criminal law. The same shall apply in regard to acts which constitute participation in, complicity in, incitement to or an attempt to commit torture.'

Article 8 states that 'Any person who alleges that he has been subjected to torture or other cruel, inhuman or degrading treatment or punishment by or at the instigation of a public official shall have the right to complain to, and to have his case impartially examined by, the competent authorities of the State concerned.'

Article 9 states that 'Wherever there is reasonable ground to believe that an act of torture as defined in article 1 has been committed, the competent authorities of the State concerned shall promptly proceed to an impartial investigation even if there has been no formal complaint.'

Article 10 states that, 'If an investigation under article 8 or article 9 establishes that an act of torture as defined in article 1 appears to have been committed, criminal proceedings shall be instituted against the alleged offender or offenders in accordance with national law. If an allegation of other forms of cruel, inhuman or degrading treatment or punishment is considered to be well founded, the alleged offender or offenders shall be subject to criminal, disciplinary or other appropriate proceedings.'

Article 11 states that, 'Where it is proved that an act of torture or other cruel, inhuman or degrading treatment or punishment has been committed by or at the instigation of a public official, the victim shall be afforded redress and compensation in accordance with national law.'

Article 12 states that, 'Any statement which is established to have been made as a result of torture or other cruel, inhuman or degrading treatment or punishment may not be invoked as evidence against the person concerned or against any other person in any proceedings.'

For the full text of this document, follow links at **www.unhchr.org**

Human Rights Organisations Concerned with Torture: UN, Regional-Governmental and NGO

1. UN: Office of the High Commissioner for Human Rights (OHCHR) Committee against Torture

The main UN body responsible for oversight of allegations of torture is the OHCHR Committee against Torture (CAT). The work of the Committee differs from the Special Rapporteur on Torture:

> The Committee considers the mandate conferred upon it by the Convention and the mandate conferred on the Special Rapporteur by the Commission on Human Rights to be different but complementary. The Rapporteur is required to report to the Commission on the phenomenon of torture in general. To that end, he asks Governments for information on the legislative and administrative measures taken to prevent torture and to remedy its consequences whenever it occurs. He also visits certain regions of the world to hold consultations with government representatives who express the wish to meet him. His task extends to all States Members of the United Nations and to all States with observer status: from that point of view, it is broader than that of the Committee.

The more detailed functions of the Special Rapporteur on Torture are explained in the *UN Human Rights Fact Sheet No. 4: Methods of Combating Torture* (UN, 2002). The Committee was established in the light of article 17 of the Convention and began its work of monitoring the Convention on 1 January 1988. The Committee consists of ten 'experts of high moral standing and recognized competence in the field of human rights'. Members of the Committee – who in normal circumstances meet twice a year – are elected by secret ballot and serve for a term of four years but are eligible for re-election.

The UN Fact Sheet No. 17 provides the best overview of the work of the Committee against Torture and one of the most succinct statements of the ideals of the Convention:

> The eradication of the practice of torture in the world was one of the major challenges taken up by the United Nations only a few years after its establishment. In order to ensure adequate protection for all persons against torture and other cruel, inhuman or degrading treatment or punishment, over the years the United Nations has adopted universally applicable standards. These standards were ultimately embodied in international declarations and conventions. The adoption on 10 December 1984 by the General Assembly of the United Nations of the Convention against Torture and Other Cruel, Inhuman or Degrading Treatment or Punishment rounded off the codification process to combat the practice of torture.
>
> In developing this valuable instrument, the United Nations did not merely put in writing in a series of articles a body of principles and pious hopes, the implementation and observance of which would not be guaranteed by anything or anyone. It set up also a monitoring body, the Committee against Torture, whose main function is to ensure that the Convention is observed and implemented. (UN 2002a)

One of the roles of the Committee is to monitor the implementation by States of the Convention. It has powers of investigation in pursuance of allegations of the systematic practice of torture. There are two basic principles of procedure here. These are set out in article 20 of the Convention: confidentiality and 'the pursuit of cooperation with the States Parties concerned'. There is a technical possibility of the accused State not recognising the competence of the Committee, in which case, 'and so long as that reservation has not been withdrawn, the Committee may not exercise the powers conferred upon it under article 20 in respect of that State Party'. Where the competence of the Committee is recognised, the gathering of information takes place according to those principles of confidentiality and cooperation of the State concerned. Accordingly, if it appears to the Committee 'that the information received is reliable and contains well founded indications that torture is being systematically practised in the territory of a State Party to the Convention, the Committee invites that State to cooperate in its examination of the information and, to this end, to submit observations with regard to that information'. Additional information can also be requested from parties concerned.

Inquiry procedures may include visit by members of the Committee to the State concerned for the gathering of further information or to hear from witnesses:

> The designated members submit their findings to the Committee, which transmits them, together with its own comments or suggestions, to the State Party. It invites that State to inform the Committee of the action it takes with regard to the Committee's findings. After all the proceedings regarding an inquiry have been completed, the Committee may decide to include a summary account of the results of the proceedings in its annual report. Only in that case is the work of the Committee made public; otherwise, all the work and documents relating to its functions under article 20 are confidential. (UN, 2002a)

Where one State claims than another is not discharging its duties under the Convention such complaints mentioned are 'subordinated to the recognition by those States of the competence of the Committee'. This suggests that domestic remedies must have been unsuccessful before recourse to the Committee.

The Committee also deals, in closed session, with complaints of individuals against States:

> Like other international instruments relating to human rights, the Convention on Torture gives private individuals, in certain circumstances, the right to lodge with the Committee complaints regarding the violation of one or more of its provisions by a State Party. For the Committee to be able to admit and examine individual communications against a State Party, its competence in that regard must however have been expressly recognized by the State concerned. (UN, 2002a)

In addition to providing an outline of the work of the Committee, the *Fact Sheet* contains a number of useful annexes:

I. Convention against Torture and Other Cruel, Inhuman or Degrading Treatment or Punishment

II. List of States which have signed or ratified the Convention against Torture and Other Cruel, Inhuman or Degrading Treatment or Punishment

III. Declarations made under articles 21 and 22 of the Convention against Torture and Other Cruel, Inhuman or Degrading Treatment or Punishment as at 1 January 1992

IV. Composition of the Committee against Torture

V. Model communication

The 'Model Communication' is reproduced in Figure 3.5.

There are strict conditions for admissibility of communications. They must not be anonymous, for example, and again, it suggests that domestic remedies must have been exhausted. Obviously, if a State is allegedly involved in torture, complaints by an individual and any 'domestic remedy' may be difficult.

Figure 3.5

Committed against Torture: Annex V

Model communication

Date: . . . .

Communication to:

The Committee against Torture
c/o Centre for Human Rights
United Nations Office
8–14 Avenue de la Paix
1211 Geneva 10
Switzerland

submitted for consideration under the Convention against Torture and Other Cruel, Inhuman or Degrading Treatment or Punishment

I. Information concerning the author of the communication

Name .... First name(s) ....

Nationality .... Profession ....

Date and place of birth ....
Present address

....

Address for exchange of confidential correspondence (if other than present address)

Submitting the communication as:

(a) Victim of the violation or violations set forth below .... [ ]

(b) Appointed representative/legal counsel of the alleged victim(s)

. ...[ ]

(c) Other .... [ ]

If box (c) is marked, the author should explain:

(i) In what capacity he is acting on behalf of the victim(s) (e.g. family relationship or other personal links with the alleged victim(s)):

....

(ii) Why the victim(s) is (are) unable to submit the communication himself (themselves):

An unrelated third party having no link to the victim(s) cannot submit a communication on his (their) behalf.

II. Information concerning the alleged victim(s) (if other than author)

Name ....

First name(s) ....

Nationality ....

Profession ....

Date and place of birth ....

Present address or whereabouts ....

III. State concerned/articles violated/domestic remedies
Name of the State party (country) to the Convention against Torture and Other Cruel, Inhuman or Degrading Treatment or Punishment against which the communication is directed:

....

Articles of the Convention against Torture allegedly violated:

....

Steps taken by or on behalf of the alleged victim(s) to exhaust domestic remedies – recourse to the courts or other public authorities,when and with what results (if possible, enclose copies of all relevant judicial or administrative decisions):
. . . .

If domestic remedies have not been exhausted, explain why:
. . . .

IV. Other international procedures
Has the same matter been submitted for examination under another procedure of international investigation or settlement (e.g. the Inter-American Commission on Human Rights, the European Commission on Human Rights)? If so, when and with what results?
. . . .

V. Facts of the claim
Detailed description of the facts of the alleged violation or violations (including relevant dates)*
Author's signature: . . . .

---

* For the full text and procedures on how to contact OHCHR, follow links at **www.un.ohchr.org**

---

2. REGIONAL-GOVERNMENTAL: Foreign and Commonwealth Office (FCO) (UK)

The Foreign and Commonwealth Office is a department of the UK government. Its Internet site is highly international in scope and contains details for travel in countries worldwide in relation to issues from safety of British subjects abroad to foreign policy. Relevant sections of the website for human rights are the 'Regional' and 'Global' sections of foreign policy. The 'Regional' structure takes the (exemplars only) outline format as in Figure 3.6: human rights highlighted in bold but cross-referenced across all domains.

Figure 3.6

FCO Foreign Policy: Regional

• Country Profiles (a global overview)

• Policy on Africa (an example of a continental overview)
    British Policy
    New Partnership for Africa's Development
    UK Conflict Prevention Initiative
    Sierra Leone: Attempts to Restore Peace
    Zimbabwe: UK Approach to Land Reform

• Policy on Latin America and Caribbean (another FCO continental overview)
    Country Profiles
    Britain and the Caribbean: A Special Relationship
    BBC World Service

British Council
Development Assistance
Drugs
Environment
Human Rights
Rio Declaration

- Relations with Iraq (an example of relation with a particular State)
    The Iraqi Threat
    Iraq's Obligations
    Iraq's Choice
    Oil for Food
    Human Rights
    Myths and Facts
    Northern Iraq
    British Help for Iraq

- Middle East Peace Process (an example of FCO in a particular regional conflict)
    Frequent Questions and Answers
    Historical Background
    Recent Policy Issues

- Policy on Western Balkans (an example of European intervention)
    SE Europe
    Stability Pact
    UK Conflict Prevention Initiative

Further details at **www.fco.gov.uk**

Each of the above has a 'News' and 'Useful Links' connection. Abuses such as torture are amongst the most self-evident of human rights infringements. Human rights reports highlights by the FCO target and report on such abuses. The FCO also represents diplomatic mission. Unlike independent NGOs, reporting of human rights abuses, almost of necessity, is filtered by diplomatic considerations and political expediency. Governments of all shades have tended to overlook human rights abuses such as torture when States performing such abuses on its own people is needed as an ally in time of war or international crisis. The recent war on terror is an example where the foreign policies of many Western governments lessened critiques of harsh and dictatorial regimes, onwards from the initial onslaught on Afghanistan.

The global section of the Foreign and Commonwealth Office is also of interest. Some of the major headings are shown in Figure 3.7.

Figure 3.7

FCO Foreign Global Policies

- Environment
    - Biodiversity
    - Climate Change
    - Sustainable Development and Globalisation
- **Human Rights**
- International Crime
- International Organisations
- Commonwealth
- Council of Europe
- European Union
- G8
- NATO
- OSCE
- United Nations
- International Security
- Global Economy
    - Corporate Citizenship

Further details at **www.fco.gov.uk**

Again, explicit mention of human rights (in bold above) is an indication of how these are important to foreign policy but their prevalence extends through cross-referencing to all other aspects of this, from environment to global economy and corporate citizenship. Human rights, at least nominally, integrate within UK government foreign policy at both regional and global levels. Foreign policy is influenced, to a greater and greater extent (again, at least in principle), to improvements in the most basic of human rights such as the right to be free from torture.

3. NON-GOVERNMENT ORGANISATION: Amnesty International (AI)

Amnesty International (AI) is probably the world's most famous human rights organisation and has for many decades propagated high profile campaigns aimed at the elimination of torture. British lawyer Peter Benenson launched an 'Appeal for Amnesty '61' with the publication of an article, 'The Forgotten Prisoners' in *The Observer* on 28 May 1961. The article was inspired by the imprisonment of two Portuguese students who had raised wine glasses in a toast for freedom. Benenson's appeal for amnesty gained worldwide publicity and was to inspire the launch of Amnesty as an organisation. That July the first international meeting was held with delegates from Belgium, UK, France, Germany, Ireland, Switzerland and the United States, establishing 'a permanent international movement in defence of freedom of opinion and religion'.

In the same year, an office and library staffed by volunteers opened in Mitre Court, London, with a 'Threes Network' established whereby each AI group adopted three prisoners from 'contrasting geographical and political areas, thus emphasizing impartiality of the group's work'. On Human Rights Day, 10 December, 1961, the first Amnesty candle was lit in the church of St Martins-in-the-Fields, London.

The Amnesty website provides a detailed timeline of Amnesty's history to date. What is noticeable, apart from its now huge international membership and its broad and popular and even celebrity appeal, is the almost instantaneous growth of the organisation. With a minimal first year expenditure of £6,040, by 1962, groups were started in Australia, Belgium, Denmark, France, Holland, Ireland, Italy, Norway, Sweden, Switzerland, the United States and West Germany. In 1962, it sent an observer to the trial of Nelson Mandela; by 1963 there were 350 Amnesty groups and today the membership exceeds one million worldwide. In August 1964, the United Nations gave Amnesty International consultative status, followed by consultative status with UNESCO in 1969. Its early effectiveness, according to its own figures is clear: in 1968 of '4,000 prisoners adopted since AI was founded, 2,000 released'. In 1972, Amnesty launched the first of many subsequent worldwide campaigns for the abolition of torture. Its timing is of interest. It was not until 1975 that the UN adopted its own Declaration against Torture. In 1978, AI was awarded the Nobel Peace Prize for its 'outstanding contributions in the field of human rights'.

Of direct and broad relevance to NGOs like AI, the Association for the Prevention of Torture – **www.apt.ch/cat/guidelines** – presents 'Guidelines for National NGOs on Alternative Reporting to UN Treaty Bodies, including the Committee against Torture'.

References, Further Reading and Research

Amnesty International (2001) *Broken Bodies, Shattered Minds: Torture and Ill-Treatment of Women* (London: Amnesty International)

Amnesty International (2001) *Crime of Hate, Conspiracy of Silence: Torture and Ill-Treatment based on Sexual Identity* (London: Amnesty International)

Amnesty International (2001) *End Impunity: Justice for Victims of Torture* (London: Amnesty International)

Amnesty International (2001) *Stopping the Torture Trade* (London: Amnesty International)

Amnesty International (2002) *Doctors and Torture* (London: Amnesty International)

Bruce-Mitford, Miranda (ed) (2001) *Torture Survivors' Perceptions of Reparation: Preliminary Survey* (London: Redress)

Bruce-Mitford, Miranda (ed) (2001) *Coalition of International Non-Governmental Organisations against Torture* London: CINAT

Cherrington, Michael (2001) *History of Torture*, Lancet, 358: 9281 (18 August)

Conroy, John (2001) *Unspeakable Acts, Ordinary People: The Dynamics of Torture* (London: Vision Paperbacks)

Gerrity, Ellen T., Terence M. Keane and Farris Tuma (eds) (2001) *The Mental Health Consequences of Torture* (New York: Kluwer)

Graessner, Stepp, Norbert Gurris and Christian Pross (eds) (2001) *At the Side of Torture Survivors: Treating a Terrible Assault on Human Dignity* (Baltimore: Johns Hopkins University Press)

Ingelse, Chris (2001) *The UN Committee Against Torture* (London: Kluwer)

Maio, Giovanni (2001) *History of Medical Involvement in Torture: Then and Now Lancet*, 357: 9268 (19 May)

Man, Nathalie (2000) *Children, Torture and Power: The Torture of Children by States and Armies* (London: Save the Children)

Morgan, Rodney and Malcolm Evans (2001) *Combating Torture: The Work and Standards of the European Committee for the Prevention of Torture* (Strasbourg: Council of Europe)

Peel, Michael (ed) (2002) *The Medical Documentation of Torture* (London: Greenwich Medical Media)

UN (2002) *Methods of Combating Torture*, Fact Sheet No. 4 (New York: United Nations)

UN (2002a) *The Committee Torture*, Fact Sheet No. 17 (New York: United Nations)

CHAPTER FOUR

Asylum

Everyone has the right to seek and to enjoy in other countries asylum from persecution.
Article 14, Universal Declaration of Human Rights

The images were stark and shocking: in the heart of Europe, tens of thousands of people were fleeing terror and murder, inflicted by their own government, because of their ethnic background. Men, women and children, bundled in blankets and carrying whatever possessions they could fit into bags, in search of safety. These images were eerily reminiscent of an earlier era, though they were not in the grainy black-and-white of the mid-1940s; rather, they were in colour and transmitted live into every TV-owning household around the world from Kosovo and the Balkan region.
Marilyn Achiron *A 'Timeless' Treaty Under Attack*

Figure 4.1

Asylum: Chapter Headings

Background Notes: Defining Asylum and Refugee Status

In historical context, Article 14 of the Universal Declaration of Human Rights – the right to asylum – reflected one particular situation in world history. In the months before the Second World War, Britain and many other countries began to close its borders to mass immigrants from Nazi Germany. The Third Reich had allowed some emigration of Jews – at a high price. Jews were taxed heavily for the privilege and the money from this gained much needed resources for the growing war machine. Jewish people and those of Jewish descent already abroad at the time of Hitler's pledge to purify the Fatherland acquired, or at least applied for, citizenship of the countries in which they resided. The philosopher Ludwig Wittgenstein – who came from one of the wealthiest families in Austria and whose family only just escaped with their lives to America – adopted British citizenship. Albert Einstein adopted American citizenship. There are innumerable other examples of notable and even famous people to whom this applied and whose contributions to their adopted countries and indeed the world were immense (Refugee Council, 2002).

Some ordinary people also managed to escape from Nazi terror. With the liberation of Auschwitz, Belsen and other death camps throughout Europe, the facts of the Holocaust began fully to emerge, and it became clear what many must surely have realised: that those who had not managed to escape were unlikely to have survived. Confirmation of this brought some sense of guilt in the victors, and perhaps most poignant were ships crammed with pre-War refugees that were returned to Nazi-controlled territory. Article 14 of Universal Declaration reflects, like UN statements on genocide, a 'never-again' form of thinking.

International Legal Standards: Defending the Right to Asylum

Given the historical context of the Universal Declaration of Human Rights, and the human rights culture that developed in subsequent decades, the right to asylum remains a fundamental civil and political right. (Basic human rights are indivisible – refugees are entitled to all other economic, social and cultural rights.) But the world of 1948 is not the same as a twenty-first century. Figures 4.2 and 4.3 give some idea of the scope of international legal standards in the field of asylum and refugee status. In the immediate post-War period, a world full of displaced peoples, refugees, especially in Europe, were a major issue. Indeed, it is part of the forgotten history of some major aid organisations, such as Christian Aid, that started life to cater for the problems of refugees in Europe before the creation of terms like the developing or Third World were created. Yet today, increasingly urgent questions relating to immigration make the human right to asylum and refugee status probably the most contested and controversial of all human rights. Figure 4.2 gives some sense of the range of international standards directed at the issue.

Figure 4.2

Asylum and Refugees

International Human Standards: Defending the Right to Asylum

Statute of the Office of the United Nations High Commissioner for Refugees (14 December 1950)

Convention relating to the Status of Refugees (28 July 1951, into effect 22 April 1954)

Convention relating to the Status of Stateless Persons (28 September 1954, into effect 6 June 1960)

Convention on the Nationality of Married Women (29 January 1957, into effect 11 August 1958)

Protocol relating to the Status of Refugees (18 November 1966, into effect 4 October 1967)

Declaration on Territorial Asylum (14 December 1967)

Convention on the Reduction of Statelessness (30 August 1961, into effect 13 December 1975)

Declaration on the Human Rights of Individuals Who are not Nationals of the Country in which They Live (13 December 1985)

For the texts of these all these documents, follow the links on **www.unhchr.ch**

Two major factors that lead persons to seek asylum are persecution within their own country and war. The context of Afghanistan before and directly after September 11 illustrates this starkly. A briefing paper on refugees before and after September 11, from the New York-based Human Rights Watch highlights the issues. In *No Safe Refuge: The Impact of the September 11 Attacks on Refugees, Asylum Seekers and Migrants in the Afghanistan Region and Worldwide*, a Human Rights Watch Backgrounder published on October 18, 2001, comments on a chronic refugee and humanitarian situation in Afghanistan and Bordering States:

> Twenty years of foreign invasion and civil war, political turmoil, continuing human rights abuses and recent drought had already displaced more than five million of Afghanistan's 27 million people before the September 11 attacks on the United States. Some four million refugees had been displaced to neighbouring countries and across the world, while a further one million people had been internally displaced within Afghanistan. (HRW: 2001)

Although the war in Afghanistan lasted a lot longer than many were predicting at the time, initial forecasts by Human Rights Watch on humanitarian crisis were initially far from optimistic. They predicted that:

> If the humanitarian situation was bad for Afghan civilians, displaced persons, and refugees before the September 11 attacks on the US, it only worsened in the four weeks afterwards. The commencement of US and British air strikes against Afghanistan on October 7 has heightened the humanitarian crisis. By early October 2001, conditions inside Afghanistan had deteriorated dramatically and aid agencies were warning of an impending humanitarian disaster. The withdrawal of all international relief agency staff after the September 11 attacks, when the Taliban declared that it could no longer guarantee their security, exacerbated an already dire situation. At the same time, the UN has reported that the Taliban have confiscated food supplies from the United Nations and relief agencies and shut down UN and NGO communication networks. As a result, many relief agencies report that they have been unable to contact their local staff in Afghanistan and obtain accurate information about conditions for the civilian population. (HRW, 2001)

The close of borders in countries neighbouring Afghanistan – China, Iran, Pakistan, Tajikistan, Turkmenistan, Uzbekistan – 'on security grounds' and 'an inability to absorb more refugees' added to fears for those seeking asylum.

In addition to persecution and war, economic factors play a part in human migration. The International Labour Organisation (ILO) estimates that up to 80 million of these are migrant workers. In 1997, ILO estimated that the number of migrant workers was as follows: Africa, 20 Million; North America, 17 million; Central and South America 12 million; Asia 7 million; the Middle East (Arab countries), 9 million, and Europe 30 million (**www.ilo.org**). Economic factors, however, are not sufficient reasons to justify refugee status nor for asylum to be granted. Yet the situations of migrant workers, a separate but not unrelated issues to that of refugees (since the two are often muddled together), often raises serious human rights issues. As the International Labour Organisation has monitoring indicates, migrants are more likely to be subject to abuses of their fundamental rights by nature of their temporary statelessness. It reports:

> Migration is hardly a recent or localised phenomenon. Women and men have been leaving their homelands in search of a better job and a life elsewhere since payment in return for labour was introduced. People also leave their own countries because of civil conflicts and insecurity or persecution. However, in this globalised world, we are witnessing an unprecedently high labour mobility and an increasing pressure of migration . . . Women and children account for more than half of the refugees and internally displaced persons, and their proportion is increasing in the case of other categories of migrants. 96 per cent of children who work and sleep in the street are migrants about half of them girls aged between 8 and 14. (HRW, 2002)

Featured Document: The 1951 Refugee Convention

The 1951 Refugee Convention, along with the basic protections of the UDHR, is the founding statement of internationally accepted norms for asylum and refugees status. Article 1 of the 1951 Refugee Convention defines a refugee as:

> A person who is outside his/her country of nationality or habitual residence; has a well-founded fear of persecution because of his/her race, religion, nationality, membership in a particular social group or political opinion; and is unable or unwilling to avail himself/herself of the protection of that country, or to return there, for fear of persecution.

Defining and protecting the rights had begun with the work of the League of Nations before the Second World War. It was six years after that war, on 28 July 1951, when a UN approved the Convention Relating to the Status of Refugees. At the beginning of the same year, the United Nations had created the High Commission for Refugees (UNHCR). The Convention defines the rights and responsibilities of refugees in relation to the State in which asylum is sought. It also outlines the responsibilities of States in the protection of the rights of refugees and the conditions for exemption to the Convention. War criminals, for example, do not qualify for refugee status. According to UNHCR's own figures, the Convention has helped to protect over 50 million refugees, including 20 million current refugees around the world today.

The 1951 Convention, summarised in Figure 4.3 is directed primarily at the protection of post-Second World War Europeans. A 1967 Protocol widened the focus of the Convention globally. Regionally, other instruments ensued, including the 1969 Africa Refugee Convention and the 1984 Latin American Cartagena Declaration. Today, however, especially, ironically, in the continental birthplace of the Convention, its contemporary appropriateness has increasingly been called into question. The UNHCR has done much work in recent years to shore up what it calls a 'timeless convention' that is now being questioned by the States that brought it into being. Yet there is strong defence of the Convention from official sources. Figure 4.3 highlights some of the contemporary questions and concerns arising over half a century since the Convention was ratified.

Figure 4.3

A Timeless Convention Brought into Question

Given the controversy over asylum seekers in many of the world's wealthiest countries, UNHCR have attempted to address some of the central questions raised in this, amongst the most challenged of all universal human rights. Here are some of the most of the important questions and the official responses.

What is contained in the 1951 Convention?

It defines what the term 'refugee' means. It outlines a refugee's rights including such things as freedom of religion and movement, the right to work, education and accessibility to travel documents, but it also underscores a refugee's obligations to a host government. A key provision stipulates that refugees should not be returned, or *refouled*, to a country where he or she fears persecution. It also spells out people or groups of people who are not covered by the Convention.

What is contained in the 1967 Protocol?

It removes the geographical and time limitations written into the original Convention under which mainly Europeans involved in events occurring before 1 January 1951 could apply for refugee status.

Is the Convention still relevant for the new millennium?

Yes. It was originally adopted to deal with the aftermath of World War II in Europe and growing East–West political tensions. But though the nature of conflict and migration patterns have changed in the intervening decades, the Convention has proved remarkably resilient in helping to protect an estimated 50 million people in all types of situations. As long as persecution of individuals and groups persists, there will be a need for the Convention.

Is the Convention meant to regulate migratory movements?

No. Millions of 'economic' and other migrants have taken advantage of improved communications in the last few decades to seek new lives in other, mainly western, countries. However, they should not be confused, as they sometimes are, with *bona fide* refugees who are fleeing life-threatening persecution and not merely economic hardship. Modern migratory patterns can be extremely complex and contain a mix of economic migrants, genuine refugees and others. Governments face a daunting task in separating the various groupings and treating genuine refugees in the appropriate manner through established and fair asylum procedures.

How are refugees and economic migrants different?

An economic migrant normally leaves a country voluntarily to seek a better life. Should he or she elect to return home they would continue to receive the protection of their government. Refugees flee because of the threat of persecution and cannot return safely to their homes in the circumstances then prevailing.

Does the Convention cover internally displaced persons?

Not specifically. Refugees are people who have crossed an international border into a second country seeking sanctuary. Internally displaced persons (IDPs) may have fled for similar reasons, but remain within their own territory and thus are still subject to the laws of that state. In specific crises, UNHCR assists several million, but not all, of the estimated 20–25 million IDPs worldwide. There is widespread international debate currently under-way on how this group of uprooted people can be better protected and by whom.

Can a soldier be a refugee?
A refugee is a civilian. Former soldiers may qualify, for instance, but a person who continues to take part in military activities cannot be considered for asylum.

Are some countries, such as those in Europe, being swamped by asylum seekers?
Countries around the world, including some in Europe, believe they are being overwhelmed by asylum seekers. And while it is true that numbers have increased inexorably in the last few decades in many areas, the concerns of individual states are all relative. The bottom line is that some nations in Africa and Asia with far fewer economic resources than industrialized countries sometimes host larger numbers of refugees for far longer periods of time.

But does the very fact of accession to the Convention provide a 'pull' factor for increasing numbers of asylum seekers?
No. Some states hosting the largest refugee populations are not parties to refugee instru-ments. Geopolitical considerations or family links play a more crucial role as far as 'attrac-tiveness' of destination is concerned.

For the full text visit links at **www.unhcr.org**

The 1951 Convention is a relatively long document. Figure 4.4 is a summary.

Figure 4.4

Featured Document: 1951 Convention relating to the Status of Refugees

Chapter I is concerned with General Provisions.
Article I defines a refugee as someone who, 'owing to well-founded fear of being persecuted for reasons of race, religion; nationality, membership of a particular social group or political opinion' is outside the country of their nationality and who 'is unable or, owing to such fear, is unwilling' to avail her/himself 'of the protection of that country; or who, not having a nationality and being outside the country of his/her former habitual residence as a result of such events, is unable or, owing to such fear, is unwilling to return to it'. But the persons to whom the Convention refers are specifically those who are so in fear of persecu-tion 'as a result of events occurring before I January 1951'. This refers to a singular, European context. 'For the purposes of this Convention, the words "events occurring before I January 1951" shall be understood to mean either (a) "events occurring in Europe before 2 January 1951"; or (b) "events occurring in Europe or elsewhere before I January 1951," and each Contracting State shall make a declaration at the time of signature,

ratification or accession, specifying which of these meanings it applies for the purpose of its obligations under this Convention.' Article 1 also provides various provisos and exceptions to refugee status and entitlement to protection, including the exclusion of the protection for anyone who has 'committed a crime against peace, a war crime, or a crime against humanity, as defined in the international instruments drawn up to make provision in respect of such crimes' or 'committed a serious non-political crime outside the country of refuge prior to his admission to that country as a refugee.'

Article 2 presents obligation for the asylum seeker. 'Every refugee has duties to the country in which he finds himself, which require in particular that he conform to its laws and regulations as well as to measures taken for the maintenance of public order.'

Article 3 states that the provisions of the Convention 'shall apply the provisions of this Convention to refugees without discrimination as to race, religion or country of origin'.

Article 4 outlines the obligation of Contracting States to 'accord to refugees within their territories treatment at least as favourable as that accorded to their nationals with respect to freedom to practice their religion and freedom as regards the religious education of their children'.

Article 5 is a statement of the indivisibility of human rights in that 'Nothing in this Convention shall be deemed to impair any rights and benefits granted by a Contracting State to refugees apart from this Convention.'

Article 6 defines 'in the same circumstances' as implying that 'any requirements (including requirements as to length and conditions of sojourn or residence) which the particular individual would *have to fulfil* for the enjoyment of the right in question if he were not a refugee, must be fulfilled . . . with the exception of requirements which by their nature a refugee is incapable of fulfilling'.

Article 7 outlines the obligations of contracting states to provide refugees with the same basic treatment as accorded to aliens generally.

Article 8 states that, 'With regard to exceptional measures which may be taken against the person, property or interests of nationals of a foreign State, the Contracting States shall not apply such measures to a refugee who is formally a national of the said State solely on account of such nationality. Contracting States which, under their legislation, are prevented from applying the general principle expressed in this article, shall, in appropriate cases, grant exemptions in favour of such refugees.'

Article 9 states that, 'Nothing in this Convention shall prevent a Contracting State, in time of war or other grave and exceptional circumstances, from taking provisional measures which it considers to be essential to the national security in the case of a particular person, pending a determination by the Contracting State that that person is in fact a refugee and that the continuance of such measures is necessary in his/her case in the interests of national security.'

Article 10 defines 'continuity of residence'. 'Where a refugee has been forcibly displaced during the Second World War and removed to the territory of a Contracting State and is resident there, the period of such enforced sojourn shall be considered to have been lawful residence within that territory.'

CHAPTER II is concerned with Legal Status.

Article 12 states that the 'personal status of a refugee shall be governed by the law of the country of his domicile or, if he has no domicile, by the law of the country of his residence'. 'Rights previously acquired by a refugee and dependent on personal status, more particularly rights attaching to marriage, shall be respected by a Contracting State.'

Article 13 deals with property rights that oblige states to accord a refugee 'treatment as favourable as possible and, in any event, not less favourable than that accorded to aliens generally in the same circumstances'. It also concerns artistic rights and industrial property and treats of 'the protection of industrial property, such as inventions, designs or models, trade marks, trade names, and of rights in literary, artistic, and scientific works'.

Article 14 state that in 'the territory of any other Contracting State' the refugee 'shall be accorded the same protection as is accorded in that territory to nationals of the country in which he has his habitual residence'.

Article 15 deals with rights of association 'as regards non-political and non-profit-making associations and trade unions, the Contracting States shall accord to refugees lawfully staying in their territory the most favourable treatment accorded to nationals of a foreign country, in the same circumstances'.

Article 16 states that a refugee shall have 'free access to the courts of law on the territory of all Contracting States' and 'enjoy in the Contracting State in which he has his habitual residence the same treatment as a national'.

Chapter III concerns employment, including wage-earning employment (**Article 17**), self-employment (**Article 18**) and employment within the 'liberal professions' (**Article 19**),

Chapter IV concern welfare, including access to rationing (**Article 20**), housing (**Article 21**), public education (**Article 22**), public relief (**Article 23**), labour legislation and social security (**Article 24**).

Chapter V concerns administrative measures, including the right to administrative assistance (**Article 25**), freedom of movement (**Article 26**), identity papers (**Article 27**), travel documents (**Article 28**). It also refers to fiscal charges, and the right not to be charged higher than usual duties and taxes for nationals (**Article 29**), and guidelines on the transfer of assets (**Article 30**). It also presents guidance on refugees unlawfully in the country of refuge (**Article 31**), expulsion (**Article 32**), prohibition of expulsion or return, known as 'refoulment' (**Article 33**) and naturalisation (**Article 34**).

Chapter VI refers to 'Executory and Transitory Provisions'. This includes state obligation to co-operate with UNHCR (**Article 35**), the provision of information on national legislation (**Article 36**), relations of the present convention to others (**Article 37**).

Chapter VII is concerned with 'Final clauses', including the settlement of disputes (**Article 38**) and procedures for signature, ratification and accession (**Article 39**). It also refers to the 'territorial application clause (**Article 40**), the 'federal clause' (**Article 41**), reservations (**Article 42**), entry into force (**Article 43**), denunciation (**Article 44**), revision (45) and notifications by the Secretary-General (**Article 46**).

For the full text, follow links at **www.unhcr.org**

Human Rights Organisations Concerned with Asylum: UN, Regional-Governmental and NGO

1. UN: United Nations High Commissioner for Refugees, Office of the (UNHCR)

The post of UN High Commissioner for Refugees was established in 1950, a year before the 1951 Refugee Convention, the office of which is based in Geneva. The League of Nations had also addressed the issue of refugees but the Second World War led to a uniquely European problem of over one million displaced persons. The UN's Relief and Rehabilitation Agency and the International Refugee Organisation paved the way for UNHCR, with a limited original mandate to address the problem of European refugees. As the 1951 Refugee Convention indicates in Article 1, it was only a strictly limited geographical region to which the Convention applied. According to UNHCR's own figures, in the first fifty years of its existence, it has given assistance to 'at least 50 million people'. In recognition of its work, UNHCR earned two Nobel Peace Prizes – in 1954 and 1981.

The High Commissioner reports on the results of the agency – working in 120 countries – to the Economic and Social Council. UNHCR deals today with those individuals as 'internally displaced persons' (IDPs), who flee their homes but not their countries, as well as those within the stricter and more narrow definition of a person who has fled their own country into another (see Article 1). Emergency relief in times of emergency such as civil war – the major cause of IDPs – takes the form of food and water, shelter and sanitation, as well as medical welfare. In parallel to long term and emergency relief, UNHCR also developed the concept of 'quick impact programmes' or QIPs, which it describes as 'usually small-scale programmes to rebuild schools and clinics, repair roads, bridges and wells'. These and other such projects are 'designed to bridge the gap between emergency assistance provided to refugees and people returning home and longer-term development aid undertaken by other agencies'. Figure 4.5 outlines some of the concrete ways UNHCR has helped refugees and internally displace persons around the world.

Figure 4.5

Where the UNHCR helps

THE BALKANS: An estimated 1.8 million civilians have returned to their home countries in the Balkans in the last few years and democratic governments were established in Yugoslavia and Croatia. But another 1.3 million persons remain displaced and throughout the first months of 2001, the former Yugoslav Republic of Macedonia teetered on the edge of full-scale insurrection.

COLOMBIA: Since 1985, nearly two million Colombians have become exiles in their own country, trying to escape a war being fought over land, ideology and drugs between Marxist guerrillas, right-wing paramilitary forces and the military. UNHCR's 2001 programme in Colombia aims at strengthening the country's ability to deal with its huge internally displaced population.

WEST AFRICA: Population movements caused by insecurity in various parts of West Africa continue throughout the region. The conflict worsened in September 2000 when parts of Guinea bordering Sierra Leone and Liberia came under attack, causing tens of thousands of Guineans and refugees to flee, and prompted UNHCR to relocate refugees remaining in the south-western Parrot's Beak region, near the border with Sierra Leone. In the first five months of 2001, 60,000 refugees were relocated to safer camps inside Guinea.

ASYLUM IN EUROPE: Member states of the European Union have been working for several years to harmonize their asylum procedures based on the full application of the Geneva Refugee Convention. But as huge numbers of people continued to seek asylum, many governments introduced tougher laws to try to curb the flow.

CENTRAL AFRICA: Huge swathes of Central Africa remained in flames. Tanzania has the largest refugee population in Africa, mainly hosting refugees from Burundi who, at the start of 2001, were also the second largest refugee group in the world cared for by UNHCR. In May 2001, Burundi, Tanzania and UNHCR signed a tripartite agreement on the voluntary repatriation of Burundi refugees. However, the situation remains extremely volatile and the agency is not yet promoting repatriation to Burundi. In Angola, two million people had been uprooted, and the incessant conflicts between UNITA and the Angolan government have caused a steady number of refugee arrivals in neighbouring countries.

THE PALESTINIAN ISSUE: Around 3.8 million people are registered with the UN Relief and Works Agency (UNRWA), the organisation responsible for Palestinian refugees. Their future continues to be one of the most complex issues in the Middle East.

NORTH CAUCASUS: In August 2001, there were some 150,000 displaced persons from Chechnya living in Ingushetia. An estimated 250,000 people fled a Russian offensive in the separatist republic of Chechnya in 1999 and UNHCR and other aid agencies assisted them in surrounding republics.

AFGHANISTAN: Afghanistan has been embroiled in conflict for the last 21 years and despite the return of more than 4.6 million refugees, there are still some 4 million Afghans outside their homeland, while another 750,000 people are displaced due to the civil war and drought inside the country. Afghans constitute the largest single refugee population in the world of concern to UNHCR.

SRI LANKA: UNHCR assists more than 700,000 people internally displaced by the ongoing civil conflict after helping more than 100,000 civilians who had fled as refugees to India during the 1980s to return home.

TIMOR: Following the murder of three UNHCR aid workers in Atambua in September 2000, aid agencies withdrew from West Timor. The total number of returns since October 1999 is nearly 180,000. An estimated 100,000 East Timorese refugees remain in Indonesia.

East Timor degenerated into chaos following an August 1999 vote for independence from Indonesia.

HORN OF AFRICA: In May 2001, nearly one year after an intermittent war between Ethiopia and Eritrea ended,UNHCR was able to start a major repatriation operation for the return of 174,000 long-time Eritrean refugees from neighbouring Sudan. UNHCR will implement projects to meet the immediate short-term needs of returning populations.

Further details at **www.unhcr.org**

In an increasingly complex and globalised world, UNHCR expansion in the nature and extent of its programmes has led to collaboration with other UN bodies. It lists collaborators as the World Food Program (WFP), the UN Children's Fund (UNICEF), the World Health Organisation (WHO), the UN Development Program (UNDP), the Office for the Coordination of Humanitarian Affairs (OCHA) and the UN High Commissioner for Human Rights. UNHCR also actively collaborates with over 500 NGOs, including the major players in disaster and humanitarian assistance like the International Committee of the Red Cross (ICRC), the International Federation of Red Cross and Red Crescent Societies (IFRC) and the International Organisation for Migration (IOM). Figure 4.6 provides a range of useful links.

Figure 4.6

Asylum and Refugee Status: Links

United Nations High Commissioner for Refugees,
Office of the (UNHCR) – Geneva, Switzerland
www.unhcr.ch

Refworld
www.unhcr.ch/refworld

International Labour Organisation (ILO) – Geneva, Switzerland
International Labour Standards and Human Rights
www.ilo.org

United Nations Children's Fund (UNICEF) – New York, USA
www.unicef.org
Children's Rights
www.unicef.org/crc/index

The State of the World's Children 2000
www.unicef.org/sowc00/uwar2

---

2. Regional-Governmental: The Home Office (UK)

Amongst a wide range of legal and other functions, the UK Home Office has oversight of immigration and matters concerned with asylum and refugee status. As a signatory to the 1951 UN Refugee Convention (see Figure 4.4), it is obliged by that Convention to follow the agreed treatment of those seeking asylum in Britain. As the Home Office states:

> The United Kingdom has a proud tradition of providing a safe haven for genuine refugees. The UK Government is determined to ensure that genuine refugees are properly protected and that there is no incentive for people who wish to migrate for other reasons to misuse asylum procedures.

In 1999, the UK Government passed the Immigration and Asylum Act, designed as a 'fairer, faster and firmer' asylum and immigration system. The main features of the new system are outlined in Figure 4.6.

Figure 4.7

Immigration and Asylum Act 1999

The main features of the UK asylum system are as follows:

- All claims receive a fair hearing.
- Fast track processes mean that some claims (and subsequent appeals) are dealt with in about four weeks. Claimants may be detained for all or part of that time;
- All claimants have a responsibility to co-operate with the authorities considering their claim.
- Some claimants are removed to another EU member state in order to pursue their claim there, if that member state is responsible for the claim under the terms of the Dublin Convention. Some other claimants are removed in order to pursue their claim in a safe country outside the European Union.
- Asylum seekers can appeal against refusal of their application or against the granting of humanitarian protection rather than refugee status. There is now a single 'one stop' right of appeal.
- The Government is also introducing a scheme to regulate immigration advisers to prevent asylum seekers being exploited by unscrupulous or incompetent advisers.
- Those who are unsuccessful on appeal will be required to leave the UK. If necessary, they will be removed.
- Those who are recognised as refugees will be granted immediate settlement in the UK and will be helped to build a new life.

Further details at **www.homeoffice.gov.uk**

The Home Office also provides (**www.homeoffice.gov.uk**) details of appeals on human rights ground against unsuccessful claims for asylum. Partly as a response to the security issues arising from September 11, the UK government issued stricter controls on immigration in February 2002, outlined in *Secure Borders, Safe Haven: Integration with Diversity in Modern Britain.*

3. NGO: The Refugee Council

The Refugee Council, a registered charity, is the UK's foremost NGO concerned with matters of asylum and refugee status. It is a membership organisation that now contains just under 200 related groups, many of them from refugee communities. Its fundamental operational principle is that 'asylum seekers and refugees should be treated with understanding and respect'. The Refugee Council's services include:

• giving advice and support to asylum seekers and refugees to help them rebuild their lives
• working with refugee community organisations, helping them grow and serve their communities
• caring for unaccompanied refugee children to help them feel safe and supported in the UK
• offering training and employment courses to enable asylum seekers and refugees to use their skills and qualifications
• managing a residential home for young refugees
• campaigning and lobbying for refugees' voices to be heard in the UK and abroad
• keeping them high on the political agenda and discussed in the media
• producing authoritative information on refugee issues worldwide, including reports, statistics and analysis.

Full details at **www.therefugeecouncil.org.uk**

The Refugee Council's international focus has developed a strong research base for the investigation of issues leading to the exile and asylum seeking of refugees in their countries of origin. In the UK, the organisation is a major protector, in terms of advice provided to refugees of refugee rights under the 1951 Convention and 1967 Protocol. Its educational programme and resources are well adapted to human rights education within this specific field. Some of its research reports are listed in Figure 4.8.

Figure 4.8

Refugee Council: Research Reports

Poverty and Asylum in the UK (London: Refugee Council, 2002)
Joint report by Oxfam and the Refugee Council

Sri Lanka: return to uncertainty (London: Refugee Council, 2002)
Report examining current developments in the peace process in Sri Lanka peace process and the impact on refugees.

Credit to the Nation (London: Refugee Council, 2002)
Newly updated study (of a report with the same name published in 1997) traces the history of refugee settlement in the UK and looks at the benefits that refugee groups and individuals have brought and continue to bring to this country.

Refugees and Progression Routes to Employment (London: Refugee Council, 2002)
Provides model routes into employment for different refugee occupational groups.

Sri Lanka: Human Rights and Refugee Returns (London: Refugee Council, 2001)
Catalogues human rights abuses: torture, arrest, detention, disappearances and death.

Where are the Children? (London: Refugee Council, 2001)
Report on the whereabouts of unaccompanied refugee children carried out by the Refugee Council and the British Agencies for Adoption and Fostering, funded by the Diana, Princess of Wales Memorial Fund.

Changing Lives: stories of exile (London: Refugee Council, 1997)
Stories of refugees from Kenya, Ethiopia, Sudan, Afghanistan, Sierra Leone, Russia, Somalia and Iraq.

Cost of Survival: trafficking of refugees in the UK (London: Refugee Council, September 1998)
Explores ssues around the trafficking of refugees into the UK and Europe.

Creating the Conditions for Refugees to Find Work (London: Refugee Council, 1999)
Research report looking at the issues relating to the employment of refugees and asylum seekers living in Britain. It contains findings of a literature review.

Just Existence: The lives of asylum seekers who have lost entitlement to benefits in the UK (1997)
Research report examines on benefit restrictions imposed on asylum seekers. Follows the day-to-day existence of 15 asylum seekers over three months in 1996.

Killing Me Slowly: refugees and torture (London: Refugee Council, 1996)
Case study analysis of the use of torture in refugee producing countries, such as Nigeria, Iraq and Turkey.

Further details at **www.therefugeecouncil.org.uk**

References, Further Reading and Research

Audit Commission (2000) *Another Country: Implementing Dispersal under the Immigration and Asylum Act 1999* (London: Audit Commission)

Brown, Michael E. (ed) (2001) *Nationalism and Ethnic Conflict* (Cambridge, MA: MIT Press)

Conway, Martin and Jose Gotovitch (eds) *Europe in Exile: European exile Communities in Britain 1940–1945* (Oxford: Berghahn)

Hayfield, Celia (2001) *Signposts: Information for Asylum Seekers and Refugees* (London: National Information Forum)

Helton, Arthur C. (2002) *The Price of Indifference: Refugees and Humanitarian Action in the New Century* (Oxford: Oxford University Press)

HRW (2002) 'No Safe Refuge: The Impact of the September 11 Attacks on Refugees, Asylum Seekers and Migrants in the Afghanistan Region and Worldwide' (New York: HRW)

Laqueur, Walter (2001) *Generation Exodus: The Fate of Young Jewish refugees from Nazi Germany* (Hanover, NH: Brandeis University Press)

Mawson, Andrew, Rebecca Dodd and John Hilary (2000) *War Brought Us Here: Protecting Children Displaced within Their Own Countries by Conflict* (London: Save the Children)

Medawar, J.S. (2000) *Hitler's Gift: Scientists Who Fled Nazi Germany* (London: Piatkus)

Prince, Baden, Jill Rutter and Marie Kerrigan (2002) *Handbook of Education for Refugees*

Refugee Council (2002) *Credit to the Nation* (London: Refugee Council, 2002)

Robinson, Jenny (ed) *Development and Displacement* (Oxford: Open University and Oxford University Press)

Rutter, Jill (2003) *Supporting Refugee Children in Schools* (Stoke on Trent: Trentham Books)

Steiner, Niklaus (2000) *Arguing About Asylum: The Complexity of Refugee Debates in Europe* (New York and London: St Martin's Press)

UNHCR (2002) *Global Report 2001* (New York: UNHCR)

UNHCR (2002) *Repatriation and Rehabilitation* (New York: UNHCR)

UNHCR (2001) *The State of The World's Refugees* (New York: UNHCR)

UNRWA (UN Relief and Works Agency) (2000) *Palestinian Refugees* (New York: UNRWA).

UN (2002) *Human Rights and Refugees*, Fact Sheet 20 (New York: United Nations)

UN (2002) *The Rights of Migrant Workers*, Fact Sheet 24 (New York: United Nations)

UN (2002) *Internally Displaced Persons: Compilation and Analysis of Legal Norms* Human Rights Study Series No. 9 (New York: United Nations)

CHAPTER FIVE

Slavery

No one shall be held in slavery or servitude; slavery and the slave trade shall be prohibited in all their forms.
Article 4, Universal Declaration of Human Rights

Figure 5.1

Slavery: Chapter Headings

Background Notes: Defining Slavery

The preamble to the Universal Declaration of Human Rights is a discourse on the fundamental freedoms. Enslavement of a human being in any form is therefore anathema to and incompatible with any notion of human rights. The Universal Declaration begins in Article 1 with that fundamental statement that, 'All human beings are born free and equal in dignity and rights.' Clearly, for many, this remains untrue even in the modern world. Slavery is a present-day reality.

According to the United Nations 'the word slavery today covers a variety of human rights violations. In addition to traditional slavery and the slave trade, these abuses include the sale of children, child prostitution, child pornography, the exploitation of child labour, the sexual mutilation of female children, the use of children in armed conflicts, debt bondage, the traffic in persons and in the sale of human organs, the exploitation of prostitution, and certain practices under apartheid and colonial régimes.' Slavery may be formally prohibited by the 1948 Universal Declaration of Human Rights (Article 4), by the 1956 UN Supplementary Convention on the Abolition of Slavery, the Slave Trade and Institutions and Practices Similar to Slavery, and a range of other international standards. Yet, as the United Nations and NGOs like Anti-Slavery International point out, slavery continues to exist today despite also being banned by law in the countries where it is most widely practised.

The world's leading and longest standing organisation working specifically on slavery suggests that when people have the idea of slavery, an image of the past is conjured up:

> We think of the buying and selling of people, their shipment from one continent to another and the abolition of the trade in the early 1800s. Even if we know nothing about the slave trade, it is something we think of as part of our history rather than our present. But the reality is slavery continues today. Millions of men, women and children around the world are forced to lead lives as slaves. Although this exploitation is often not called slavery, the conditions are the same. People are sold like objects, forced to work for little or no pay and are at the mercy of their 'employers'. (Anti-Slavery International, 2002. Visit **www.asi.org.uk**

Anti-Slavery International defines slavery by a number of common characteristics that distinguish slavery from other human rights violations. A slave is:

- forced to work through mental or physical threat
- owned or controlled by an 'employer', usually through mental or physical abuse or threatened abuse
- dehumanised, treated as a commodity or bought and sold as 'property'
- physically constrained or has restrictions placed on his/her freedom of movement.

These are some of the forms of slavery existing today:

- Bonded labour affects at least 20 million people around the world. People become bonded labourers by taking or being tricked into taking a loan for as little as the cost of medicine for a sick child. To repay the debt, they are forced to work long hours, seven days a week, 365 days a year. They receive basic food and shelter as 'payment' for their work, but may never pay off the loan, which can be passed down through several generations.
- Forced labour affects people who are illegally recruited by governments, political parties or private individuals, and forced to work – usually under threat of violence or other penalties.
- Worst forms of child labour refers to children who work in exploitative or dangerous conditions. Tens of millions of children around the world work full-time, depriving them of the education and recreation crucial to their personal and social development.
- Commercial sexual exploitation of children. Children are exploited for their commercial value through prostitution, trafficking and pornography. They are often kidnapped, bought, or forced to enter the sex market.
- Trafficking involves the transport and/or trade of humans, usually women or children, for economic gain using force or deception. Often migrant women are tricked and forced into domestic work or prostitution.
- Early and forced marriage affects women and girls who are married without choice and forced into lives of servitude, often accompanied by physical violence.
- Traditional or 'chattel' slavery involves the buying and selling of people. They are often abducted from their homes, inherited or given as gifts.

For full details Anti-Slavery International at **www.asi.org.uk**

International Legal Standards: Defending against Slavery

From the days of abolition, and the anti-slave campaigners like Wilberforce, slavery was arguably amongst the first 'human rights' issues to attract international protest at was clearly an infringement of human dignity and liberty. While different countries have in recent centuries made the practice illegal, international efforts to outlaw slavery date to the late nineteenth and early twentieth centuries. Such moves included the 1889–90 General Act of Brussels Conference (aimed specifically at ending traffic in African slaves) and the 1919 Convention of Saint-Germain-en-Laye (revising the 1885 General Act of Berlin and the 1890 Declaration of Brussels). These attempts to suppress slavery in all its forms and banish the slave trade from land and sea were taken up by the League of Nations' Temporary Slavery Commission (appointed 1924). The 1926 Slavery Convention (which entered into force in 1927) remains the foundation for today's international standards set by the United Nations, as outlined in Figure 5.2. Later documents include Protocol amending the Slavery Convention (1953) and the Supplementary Convention on the Abolition of Slavery, the Slave Trade, and Institutions and Practices Similar to Slavery (1956). Indeed, these two documents consist of many statements that simply replace references to the League of Nations with the United Nations.

Figure 5.2

International Legal Standards: Defending against Slavery

Slavery Convention (25 September 1926, into effect 9 March 1927)

Forced Labour Convention (28 June 1930, into effect 1 May 1932)

Convention for the Suppression of the Traffic in Persons and of the Exploitation of the Prostitution of Others (2 December 1949, into effect 25 July 1951)

Protocol amending the Slavery Convention (23 October 1953, into effect 7 December 1953)

Supplementary Convention on the Abolition of Slavery, the Slave Trade, and Institutions and Practices Similar to Slavery (September 1956, into effect 30 April 1957)

Abolition of Forced Labour Convention (25 June 1957, into effect 17 January 1959)

For full texts, follow links to **www.un.unhchr.org**

Figure 5.3

Slavery Convention
(25 September 1926, into effect 9 March 1927)

Article 1 states that, for the purpose of the Convention, 'the following definitions are agreed upon:

(1) Slavery is the status or condition of a person over whom any or all of the powers attaching to the right of ownership are exercised.

(2) The slave trade includes all acts involved in the capture, acquisition or disposal of a person with intent to reduce him to slavery; all acts involved in the acquisition of a slave with a view to selling or exchanging him; all acts of disposal by sale or exchange of a slave acquired with a view to being sold or exchanged, and, in general, every act of trade or transport in slaves.'

Article 2 commits the contracting parties of the League of Nations 'each in respect of the territories placed under its sovereignty, jurisdiction, protection, suzerainty or tutelage, so far as they have not already taken the necessary steps:

(a) To prevent and suppress the slave trade
(b) To bring about, progressively and as soon as possible, the complete abolition of slavery in all its forms.'

Article 3 commits contracting parties to 'undertake to adopt all appropriate measures with a view to preventing and suppressing the embarkation, disembarkation and transport of slaves in their territorial waters and upon all vessels flying their respective flags'.

Article 4 commits contracting parties to 'give to one another every assistance with the object of securing the abolition of slavery and the slave trade'.

Article 5 commits contracting parties to recognising 'that recourse to compulsory or forced labour may have grave consequences and undertake, each in respect of the territories placed under its sovereignty, jurisdiction, protection, suzerainty or tutelage, to take all necessary measures to prevent compulsory or forced labour from developing into conditions analogous to slavery'.

Article 6 commits contracting parties 'whose laws do not at present make adequate provision for the punishment of infractions of laws and regulations enacted with a view to giving effect to the purposes of the present Convention' to 'undertake to adopt the necessary measures in order that severe penalties may be imposed in respect of such infractions'.

Article 7 commits contracting parties 'to communicate to each other and to the Secretary-General of the League of Nations any laws and regulations which they may enact with a view to the application of the provisions of the present Convention'.

Article 8 commits contracting parties to 'agree that disputes arising between them relating to the interpretation or application of this Convention shall, if they cannot be settled by direct negotiation, be referred for decision to the Permanent Court of International Justice'.

Article 9 concerns the implications for contracting parties of signing or ratifying the Convention, and the nature of the legal obligations across its territories

Article 10 concerns the denunciation of the Convention, and the procedures and implications of this.

Article 11 concerns procedures for signing the Convention, 'open for signature by the States Members of the League of Nations until April 1st, 1927', when the Secretary-General of the League of Nations 'will subsequently bring the present Convention to the notice of

States which have not signed it, including States which are not Members of the League of Nations, and invite them to accede thereto'.

Article 12 concerns the ratification and operational status of the Convention.

For the full text of the document, follow links at **www.unhchr.org**

Figure 5.4 provides some of the key aspects of the 1956 Supplementary. This adds to the 1926 Convention. Importantly, it takes the form of extending the scope of the practice of slavery to abuses of human labour that might not have come strictly under the definition of slavery in the 1926 Convention.

Figure 5.4

Featured Document

Supplementary Convention on the Abolition of Slavery, the Slave Trade, and Institutions and Practices Similar to Slavery (1956, entry into force 1957)

SECTION I: INSTITUTIONS AND PRACTICES SIMILAR TO SLAVERY

Article 1 commits States Parties to 'take all practicable and necessary legislative and other measures to bring about progressively and as soon as possible the complete abolition or abandonment' of 'institutions and practices where they still exist and whether or not they are covered by the definition of slavery contained in article 1 of the [1926] Slavery Convention':

'(a) Debt bondage, that is to say, the status or condition arising from a pledge by a debtor of his personal services or of those of a person under his control as security for a debt, if the value of those services as reasonably assessed is not applied towards the liquidation of the debt or the length and nature of those services are not respectively limited and defined;

(b) Serfdom, that is to say, the condition or status of a tenant who is by law, custom or agreement bound to live and labour on land belonging to another person and to render some determinate service to such other person, whether for reward or not, and is not free to change his status;

(c) Any institution or practice whereby:

  (i)   A woman, without the right to refuse, is promised or given in marriage on payment of a consideration in money or in kind to her parents, guardian, family or any other person or group; or
  (ii) The husband of a woman, his family, or his clan, has the right to transfer her to another person for value received or otherwise; or
  (iii) A woman on the death of her husband is liable to be inherited by another person;

(d) Any institution or practice whereby a child or young person under the age of 18 years is delivered by either or both of his natural parents or by his guardian to another person, whether for reward or not, with a view to the exploitation of the child or young person or of his labour.'

Article 2 concerns achieving 'suitable minimum ages of marriage, to encourage the use of facilities whereby the consent of both parties to a marriage may be freely expressed in the presence of a competent civil or religious authority, and to encourage the registration of marriages'.

SECTION II: THE SLAVE TRADE

Article 3 states that 'the act of conveying or attempting to convey slaves from one country to another by whatever means of transport, or of being accessory thereto, shall be a criminal offence under the laws of the States Parties to this Convention and persons convicted there-of shall be liable to very severe penalties'. There are also commitments for States to 'take all effective measures to prevent ships and aircraft authorized to fly their flags from conveying slaves and to punish persons guilty of such acts or of using national flags for that purpose and to 'take all effective measures to ensure that their ports, airfields and coasts are not used for the conveyance of slaves'.

Article 4 states that 'Any slave who takes refuge on board any vessel of a State Party to this Convention shall *ipso facto* be free.'

SECTION III: SLAVERY AND INSTITUTIONS AND PRACTICES SIMILAR TO SLAVERY

Article 5 states that 'In a country where the abolition or abandonment of slavery, or of the institutions or practices mentioned in article 1 of this Convention, is not yet complete, the act of mutilating, branding or otherwise marking a slave or a person of servile status in order to indicate his status, or as a punishment, or for any other reason, or of being accessory thereto, shall be a criminal offence under the laws of the States Parties to this Convention and persons convicted thereof shall be liable to punishment.'

Article 6 states that the act 'of enslaving another person or of inducing another person to give himself or a person dependent upon him into slavery, or of attempting these acts, or being accessory thereto, or being a party to a conspiracy to accomplish any such acts, shall be a criminal offence under the laws of the States Parties to this Convention and persons convicted thereof shall be liable to punishment'.

SECTION IV: DEFINITIONS

Article 7 presents the following definitions:

'(a) "Slavery" means, as defined in the Slavery Convention of 1926, the status or condition of a person over whom any or all of the powers attaching to the right of ownership are exercised, and "slave" means a person in such condition or status;

(b) "A person of servile status" means a person in the condition or status resulting from any of the institutions or practices mentioned in article 1 of this Convention;

(c) "Slave trade" means and includes all acts involved in the capture, acquisition or disposal of a person with intent to reduce him to slavery; all acts involved in the acquisition of a slave with a view to selling or exchanging him; all acts of disposal by sale or exchange of a person acquired with a view to being sold or exchanged; and, in general, every act of trade or transport in slaves by whatever means of conveyance.'

SECTION V: CO-OPERATION BETWEEN STATES PARTIES AND COMMUNICATION OF INFORMATION

Article 8 details the form of such co-operation.

SECTION VI: FINAL CLAUSES

Article 9 states that 'No reservations may be made to this Convention.

Article 10 concerns disputes over the Supplementary.

Article 11 concerns the signing of the Supplementary, **Article 12** its geographical application, **Article 13** its coming into force, **Article 14** its denunciation, **Article 15** its availability in translation.

For the full text, follow links at **www.unhchr.org**

Organisations Concerned with Slavery: UN/Regional-Governmental and NGO

1. UN/Regional-Governmental: International Labour Organisation (ILO)

Founded in 1919, and the only surviving creation of the Treaty of Versailles and the League of Nations, the International Labour Organisation (ILO) was the first of all specialized UN agencies created in 1946. The ILO 'seeks the promotion of social justice and internationally recognized human and labour rights'.

The mandate of the ILO is defined as formulating 'international labour standards in the form of Conventions and Recommendations setting minimum standards of basic labour rights: freedom of association, the right to organize, collective bargaining, abolition of forced labour, equality of opportunity and treatment, and other standards regulating conditions across the entire spectrum of work related issues'. It provides technical assistance primarily in the fields of:

- vocational training and vocational rehabilitation
- employment policy
- labour administration
- labour law and industrial relations
- working conditions
- management development
- cooperatives
- social security
- labour statistics and occupational safety and health.

Its scope is truly international in the field of labour relations. Since its beginnings in 1919 it has produced many conventions in the field of employment law, including important work on the exploitation of women, children and indigenous peoples. Full texts of all relevant conventions, and current campaigns, can be found at **www.ilo.org**. In terms of Slavery, its 1957 Convention against Enforced Labour marks a significant landmark in the continuing struggle against practices that characterise modern forms of the slave trade.

3. NGO: Anti-Slavery International

Founded in 1839, Anti-Slavery International, according to its own publicity, is 'the world's oldest international human rights organisation' and 'the only charity in the United Kingdom to work exclusively against slavery and related abuses'. It works 'at local, national and international levels to eliminate the system of slavery around the world' by:

* urging governments of countries with slavery to develop and implement measures to end it
* lobbying governments and intergovernmental agencies to make slavery a priority issue
* supporting research to assess the scale of slavery in order to identify measures to end it
* working with local organisations to raise public awareness of slavery
* educating the public about the realities of slavery and campaigning for its end.

Anti-Slavery divides its work into three interrelated areas of operation:

* Programme
  Working with partner organisations around the world, the programme team collects information on various forms of slavery, publishes research findings on debt bondage, forced labour, forced marriage, the worst forms of child labour, human trafficking and 'traditional slavery', campaigning for legal protection for those affected by such practices.

* Communication
  This team focuses upon campaigning, education and media relations, publishing the Anti-Slavery magazine, *The Reporter.*

* Information.
  This team focuses on fundraising, along with maintaining the Anti-Slavery reference library and archive, with extensive resources dating from the early days of the abolitionist movement through to the present.

For full details visit Anti-Slavery International at **www.asi.org**

Figure 5.5 gives some examples of Anti-Slavery International's educational materials.

Figure 5.5

Anti-Slavery's Education Resources

Anti-Slavery's education programme 'promotes human rights in schools and youth clubs throughout the UK' and 'focuses particularly on examples of contemporary and historical slavery and the international instruments used to protect human rights'.

When Rights are Left
Classroom resources linking directly to the National Curriculum at Key Stage 3. Four books cover four key subject areas: Citizenship, History, Geography and English.
Anti-Slavery International 2001.

Our News, Our Views: Children's Rights, Child Labour and the Media
Young reporters present a series of eight news stories exploring the lives of working

children in today's world. Lively and accessible, the video helps young people think about the questions and challenges they face in their lives.

Recommended for teachers of Citizenship, English, PSHE and Media Studies.

The Changing Face of Slavery
(New edition, additional information and activities)
Key Stage 3 directly linked to the National Curriculum and can be used with History, RE, PHSE, Modern Studies and English.

Diane Louise Jordan presents two human rights programmes, dramatically bringing to life slavery, past and present.

Part 1 (15 mins) investigates the Transatlantic Slave Trade, how and why it began and the arguments for and against its abolition. It encourages students to examine their understanding of slavery issues and looks at its existence in today's world.

Part 2 (15 mins) looks at children working in Britain during the Industrial Revolution, why they worked and what life was like. It links the historical with the contemporary by exploring child labour around the world today, the reasons and the alternatives. The theme of child rights runs throughout.

The pack also contains 40 pages of photocopiable support material for teachers. It raises challenging questions and introduces new ideas, helping students tackle the subjects of slavery and human rights.

Also available is a powerful exhibition in full colour exploring similar issues in greater depth. In two sizes – A1 and A3 – these 20 panels are ideal for display in classrooms, libraries or meeting halls.

Anti-Slavery International, further details at **www.asi.org**

Further Reading and Research

Bales, Kevin (2000) *Disposable People* (Berkeley: California University Press)

Davis, David Brion (2001) *In the Image of God: Religion, Moral Values and Our Heritage of Slavery* (New Haven: Yale University Press)

Engerman, Stanley, Seymour Drescher and Robert Paquette (eds) *Slavery*, Oxford readers series (Oxford; Oxford University Press)

Glancy, Jennifer A. *Slavery in Early Christianity* (Oxford: Oxford University Press)

Harmer, H.J.P. (ed) (2001) *The Longman Companion to Slavery, Emancipation and Civil Rights* (Harlow: Longman)

Haynes, Stephen R. (2002) *Noah's Curse: The Biblical Justification of American Slavery* (Oxford: Oxford University Press)

Horowitz, David (2002) *Uncivil War: The Controversy over Reparations for Slavery* (San Francisco, CA: Encounter Books)

Nitze, Paul (ed) (2002) *Human Rights Report on Trafficking in Persons, Especially Women and Children: A Country-by-Country Report on a Contemporary Form of Slavery/ The Protection Project* (Washington, DC: Johns Hopkins University)

Rohrbach, Augusta (2002) *Truth Stranger than Fiction: Race, Realism and the US Literary Marketplace* (Basingstoke: Palgrave)

Shaw, Brent (ed) (2001) *Spartacus and the Slave Wars: A Brief History with Documents* (Boston, MA: Bedford)

Shepherd, Verene A. (2002) *Working Slavery, Pricing Freedom: perspectives from the Caribbean, Africa and the African Diaspora* (Oxford: James Currey)

Tackach, James (ed) (2001) *Slave Narratives* (San Diego, CA: Greenhaven)
Tanaka, Toshiuki (2001) *Japan's Comfort Women: Sexual Slavery and Prostitution during World War II and the US Occupation* (New York: Routledge)
United Nations (2002) *Fact Sheet on Modern Slavery* (New York: United Nations)
Walvin, James (2001) *Black Ivory: A History of British Slavery* (Malden, MA: Blackwell Publishers)

II

Defining and Defending Human Rights

II
Economic, Social and Cultural Rights

CHAPTER SIX

The Right to Development

Poverty eradication without empowerment is unsustainable. Social integration without minority rights is unimaginable. Gender equality without women's rights is illusory. Full employment without workers' rights may be no more than a promise of sweatshops, exploitation and slavery. The logic of human rights in development is inescapable. Mary Robinson, United Nations High Commissioner for Human Rights

---

Figure 6.1

The Right to Development: Chapter Headings

Background Notes: Defining the Right to Development

The right to development is arguably amongst the most complex of all human rights, partly because development is so broad and thus so difficult a term to define. Several articles of the Universal Declaration are relevant. For example, Article 23 – 'Everyone has the right to work' – or Article 25 – 'Everyone has the right to a standard of living adequate for health and well-being' – or Article 26 – 'Everyone has the right to education' – or Article 27 – 'Everyone has the right freely to participate in the cultural life of the community'. All of these directly impinge upon personal and social development. Interestingly, it is Article 29 – 'Everyone has duties to the community in which alone the free and full development of his personality is possible' –

the only article to mention the idea of *duty* or *responsibility* in which the word *development* appears most prominently.

The right to development can be seen as a second-generation right (relating economic, social and cultural development) or a third-generation right (relating to questions of 'human solidarity'). In terms of UN human rights policy, it fits both second and third generation thinking – on the one hand, notions of development are fundamental to the International Covenant on Economic, Social and Cultural Development (1966). Yet, on the other, the specific UN Declaration on Development appears only in 1986, twenty years later. For a summary of key issues and events, see Figure 6.2.

Figure 6.2

Human rights in development – What is it all about?

The links between human rights and development are illustrated by the normative and operational guidance that human rights instruments, and the mechanisms established by the United Nations to monitor their implementation, provide on the right to development, rights-based approaches to development, poverty eradication, human rights mainstreaming, good governance and globalisation.

International cooperation in promoting and encouraging respect for human rights and fundamental freedoms for all is one of the purposes of the United Nations set out in Article I of the Charter. The Vienna Declaration and Programme of Action stated that 'democracy, development and respect for human rights and fundamental freedoms are interdependent and mutually reinforcing'.

The 1995 World Summit for Social Development and the Copenhagen Declaration it adopted established a new consensus on placing people at the centre of sustainable development, eradicating poverty, promoting full and productive employment, and fostering social integration in order to achieve stable, safe and just societies for all. The collective message of all the UN summits and conferences of the 1990s may be summed up as a call for greater recognition of human rights in development.

Links
World Conference on Human Rights (Vienna, 1993)
Vienna + 5

International Conference on Population and Development (Cairo, 1994)
Cairo + 5

World Summit for Social Development (Copenhagen, 1995)
Copenhagen + 5

Fourth World Conference on Women (Beijing, 1995)
Beijing + 5
World Conference against Racism, Racial Discrimination, Xenophobia and
Related Intolerance (Durban, 2001)

Rio + 10: World Summit on Sustainable Development (Johannesburg, 2–11 September 2002)

Working Group on the Right to Development (7–18 October 2002)

For a full text of the relevant documents, follow links at **www.undp.org**

'Earth Summits' such as those at Rio in 1992 and 2002 deal with such issues but the question of how to resolve disparities between the wealthy and the poverty-stricken nations highlights a fundamental contradiction in all international human rights declarations, covenants and conventions: the disparity between the stated intentions and the lived realities. This was the critical issue for all human rights in global context at the World Conference on Human Rights in 1993 and in the review five years later in 1998 by the UN Commissioner on Human Rights. It remains so today.

International Legal Standards: Defending the Right to Development

The preamble to the Declaration on the Right to Development highlights the notion of the indivisibility of all rights. It recognises that 'development is a comprehensive economic, social, cultural and political process, which aims at the constant improvement of the well-being of the entire population and of all individuals on the basis of their active, free and meaningful participation in development and in the fair distribution of benefits resulting therefrom'.

The preamble recalls the provisions of both the International Covenant on Economic, Social and Cultural Rights and the International Covenant on Civil and Political Rights, and in so doing 'the right of peoples to self-determination, by virtue of which they have the right freely to determine their political status and to pursue their economic, social and cultural development'. It also recognises 'the right of peoples to exercise, subject to the relevant provisions of both International Covenants on Human Rights, full and complete sovereignty over all their natural wealth and resources'. What would have been unthinkable in 1948, and increasingly inevitable in 1966, was the sense of historical injustice done by the presently wealthy former colonial powers so instrumental in drawing up the Universal Declaration of Human Rights. The range of post-1948 standards of relevance to the right to development is presented in Figure 6.3.

Figure 6.3

International Legal Standards: Defending the Right to Development

Universal Declaration on the Eradication of Hunger and Malnutrition (16 November 1964)

Declaration on Social Progress and Development (11 December 1969)

Declaration on the Rights of Mentally Retarded Persons (20 December 1971)

Declaration on the Use of Scientific and Technological Progress in the Interests of Peace and for the Benefit of Mankind (10 November 1975)

Declaration on the Rights of Disabled Persons (9 December 1975)

Declaration on the Right of Peoples to Peace (12 November 1984)

Declaration on the Right to Development (4 December 1986)

Guidelines for the Regulation of Computerized Personal Data Files (14 December 1990)

International Convention on the Protection of the Rights of All Migrant Workers and Members of Their Families (18 December 1990)

Principles for the protection of persons with mental illness and the improvement of mental health care (17 December 1991)

Universal Declaration on the Human Genome and Human Rights (UNESCO) (2001)

Right to enjoy culture, international cultural development and co-operation
Declaration of the Principles of International Cultural Co-operation (UNESCO) (4 November 1966)

Recommendation concerning Education for International Understanding, Co-operation and Peace and Education relating to Human Rights and Fundamental Freedoms (UNESCO) (19 November 1974)

For full texts, follow links at **www.unhchr.org**

The language of the Declaration of the Right to Development (see Figure 6.4) speaks with considerable anger at this historical and, many would argue, continuing legacy. It speaks of 'massive and flagrant violations of the human rights of the peoples and individuals' affected by 'colonialism, neo-colonialism, apartheid, all forms of racism and racial discrimination, foreign domination and occupation'. In addition, the elimination of 'aggression and threats against national sovereignty, national unity and territorial integrity and threats of war' would contribute to 'circumstances propitious to the development of a great part of mankind'.

Like other international standards, the Declaration on the Right to Development recognises that 'international peace and security are essential elements for the realisation of the right to development' and 'that there is a close relationship between disarmament and development', with progress in disarmament seen as likely to promote progress in development. It betrays an idealism when it suggests 'that resources released through disarmament measures should be devoted to the economic and social development and well-being of all peoples and, in particular, those of the developing countries'. In the final analysis, despite talk of the integrated nature of (economic, social and cultural; civil and political) rights, the right to development is crucially dependent in one way or another on finance. Thus the Declaration recognises that the 'creation of conditions favourable to the development of peoples and individuals is the primary responsibility of their States', hopes that on a global level there might be 'a new international economic order'.

Figure 6.4

Featured Document

Declaration on the Right to Development
Adopted by the UN General Assembly, 4 December 1986

Article 1 states that the right to development is 'an inalienable human right by virtue of which every human person and all peoples are entitled to participate in, contribute to, and enjoy economic, social, cultural and political development, in which all human rights and fundamental freedoms can be fully realized'. According to the Declaration this implies 'the full realisation of the right of peoples to self-determination, which includes . . . the exercise of their inalienable right to full sovereignty over all their natural wealth and resources'.

Article 2 states that 'the human person is the central subject of development and should be the active participant and beneficiary of the right to development'. Aticle 2 also speaks of the responsibility of all human being for development, 'individually and collectively' and 'duties to the community' as well as rights and freedoms. It also reiterates the responsibilities of States 'to formulate appropriate national development policies that aim at the constant improvement of the well-being of the entire population and of all individuals, on the basis of their active, free and meaningful participation in development and in the fair distribution of the benefits resulting therefrom'.

Article 3 sets forth the 'primary responsibility' of States to provide 'for the creation of national and international conditions favourable to the realisation of the right to development'. States also have 'the duty to co-operate with each other in ensuring development and eliminating obstacles to development. States should realize their rights and fulfil their duties in such a manner as to promote a new international economic order based on sovereign equality, interdependence, mutual interest and co-operation among all States, as well as to encourage the observance and realisation of human rights.'

Article 4 sets forth the responsibility of 'to take steps, individually and collectively, to formulate international development policies with a view to facilitating the full realisation of the right to development'.

Article 5 sets forth the responsibility of States to 'take resolute steps to eliminate the massive and flagrant violations of the human rights of peoples and human beings affected by situations such as those resulting from apartheid, all forms of racism and racial discrimination, colonialism, foreign domination and occupation, aggression, foreign interference and threats against national sovereignty, national unity and territorial integrity, threats of war and refusal to recognize the fundamental right of peoples to self-determination'.

Article 6 elaborates the principle that 'All States should co-operate with a view to promoting, encouraging and strengthening universal respect for and observance of all human rights and fundamental freedoms for all without any distinction as to race, sex, language or religion.' It also emphasises that 'All human rights and fundamental freedoms are indivisible and interdependent; equal attention and urgent consideration should be given to the implementation, promotion and protection of civil, political, economic, social and cultural rights.'

Article 7 sets forth the principle that 'All States should promote the establishment, maintenance and strengthening of international peace and security and, to that end, should do their utmost to achieve general and complete disarmament under effective international control, as well as to ensure that the resources released by effective disarmament measures are used for comprehensive development, in particular that of the developing countries.'

Article 8 sets forth the principle that 'States should undertake, at the national level, all necessary measures for the realisation of the right to development and shall ensure, inter alia, equality of opportunity for all in their access to basic resources, education, health services, food, housing, employment and the fair distribution of income.'

Article 9 reiterates the principle of the 'indivisible and interdependent' nature of the rights sets forth in the Declaration that 'each of them should be considered in the context of the whole'.

Article 10 sets forth the principle that 'Steps should be taken to ensure the full exercise and progressive enhancement of the right to development, including the formulation, adoption and implementation of policy, legislative and other measures at the national and international levels.'

For the full text, follow links at **www.unhchr.org**

Organisations Concerned with the Right to Development: UN, Regional-Governmental and NGO

1. UN: The United Nations Development Programme (UNDP)

UNDP is the UN's global development network 'advocating for change and connecting countries to knowledge, experience and resources to help people build a better life'. UNDP works on the ground in over 160 countries. UNDP's various networks here assist national governments to achieve the Millennium Development Goals (MDGs), including the halving of world poverty by 2015. The UNDP identifies a number of areas of strategic operation called 'Thematic Trust Funds', towards which finance and other support is directed. The Thematic Trust Funds are:

• Democratic Governance, including Project Summaries
• Poverty Reduction
• Energy
• Environment
• Information and Communications Technology
• HIV/AIDS
• Gender

These are designed as 'results-oriented programmes at the country, regional and global levels'. Across all these activities, UNDP is committed to 'the protection of human rights and the empowerment of women'. Again, we see the theory and practice of sustainable development suffused and being underpinned by the language of human rights. Figure 6.5 summarises the role of the UNDP at the World Summit on Sustainable Development.

Figure 6.5

World Summit on Sustainable Development (WSSD): UNDP's Role

Over 50,000 people were in Johannesburg to attend the World Summit on Sustainable Development (WSSD) from 26 August to 4 September 2002. UNDP is committed to ensuring that WSSD provides fresh impetus for the international sustainable development process.

As the UN's global development network, UNDP helps countries implement sustainable development principles, connecting national and local initiatives to knowledge, experience and resources from around the world. We support capacity development at the country level and regional and global cooperation to achieve the Millennium Development Goals.

- Capacity 21 and Capacity 2015
- Drylands Development Centre
- Energy for Sustainable Development
- Equator Initiative
- Poverty and Environment Initiative
- UNDP GEF and Small Grants Programme
- Water Governance
- LIFE

Johannesburg Summit promotes partnerships for development

Thursday, 5 September 20002: After twelve days of intense negotiations in Johannesburg, the World Summit on Sustainable Development concluded last night with the adoption of a political declaration and a plan of implementation to fight poverty and preserve the environment.

Over 100 Heads of State and Government attended the summit and adopted the final documents, which focused the attention of the world on five priority areas: water, energy, health, agriculture and biodiversity. Progress in these areas is essential for halving severe poverty by 2015 and achieving the other Millennium Development Goals (MDGs).

'The summit represents a major leap forward in the development of partnerships, with the UN, governments, business and civil society coming together to increase the pool of resources to tackle global problems on a global scale,' said UN Secretary-General Kofi Annan.

The world leaders reaffirmed the principles of sustainable development adopted in the Earth Summit in Rio de Janeiro 10 years ago [1992], and also affirmed the role of trade in reducing poverty agreed on at the World Trade Organisation (WTO) meeting in Doha last year and their commitments on development financing at the International Conference on Financing for Development in Monterrey, Mexico, in March.

In addition, they set a new target for reducing by half the proportion of people with no access to adequate sanitation by 2015 and recognized the link between access to energy services and poverty eradication. The governments also committed to reducing agricultural subsidies and protecting biodiversity, including in fisheries.

The summit reaffirmed the UNDP mandate for capacity building, which UNDP is pushing forward through the Capacity 2015 initiative, focusing on helping countries reach the MDGs. It also called for UNDP to provide technical assistance in trade, environment, and development, along with the WTO, the UN Conference on Trade and Development and the UN Environment Programme.

The summit emphasized the role of the private sector and civil society as key partners to achieving sustainable development and the creation of public-private partnerships to help improve the living standards of the world's poor.

Further details at **www.undp.org**

UNDP has a special role in Capacity 2015, the year-focused sustainable development programme of the UN. Capacity 2015 is based on principles of 'local and national actors' achieving 'ownership, defining their own needs and implementing their own solutions' in regard to 'urgent short-term poverty concerns and longer-term sustainability issues'. It recognises that short and long-term, such problems cannot be seen in 'isolation from one another; they require carefully integrated responses'. Here, 'Civic engagement and sound participatory processes are key elements in the design, implementation and monitoring of social, economic, and environmental policies and practices.' With sensitivity to local needs for such a global programme, the UNDP states that 'Cultural identities and values need to be recognized and respected.' The official launch of Capacity 2015 at the Fourth Session of the Preparatory Committee in Bali was controversial, mainly because of the luxury and perceived exoticism of the exclusive beach location for the assembled world leaders discussing global poverty and sustainable development. The Johannesburg Summit in September 2002 was the occasion for national leaders to announce support for the overall Capacity 2015 platform and its different areas of activity; the Bali bomb around a month later was another reminder that not all share a universal system of value. Capacity 2015's operational features and targeted outcomes are outlined in Figure 6.6.

Figure 6.6

UNDP and Capacity 2015

UNDP IS SEEKING GLOBAL. ENDORSEMENT AND SUPPORT FOR THE CAPACITY 2015 PLATFORM. Capacity 2015's overall goal is to develop the capacities needed by developing countries and countries in transition to meet their sustainable development goals under Agenda 21 and the Millennium Development Goals. It will orient and support a number of key capacity development initiatives, including developing capacities for local sustainable development, national sustainable development strategies, local capacity development for Multilateral Environmental Agreements, developing capacities to reduce vulnerability in small island developing states (SIDS) and a strategic capacity development facility. Capacity 2015, operating globally and nationally, will help developing and transition countries ensure co-ordination, mutual support and maximum synergies among partners' capacity development efforts.

The Capacity 2015 approach involves:

- Addressing local capacity development needs, tying them to national economic, social and environmental policy and processes
- Helping local groups, and their supporting local and national governments, private sectors and civil society organisations to overcome capacity constraints to achieving economic, social and environmental sustainability
- Promoting local, national, regional and global partnerships among public and private sectors and the major groups of civil society, giving each new opportunities to bring to bear on their respective strengths and resources and learn from one another
- Ensuring strong synergies among all relevant capacity development initiatives, particularly those related to multilateral environmental treaties, poverty reduction strategies and sustainable development strategies.

Expected outcomes of Capacity 2015 include the following:

- Developing countries and countries in transition accelerate their implementation of Agenda 21 and their achievement of the Millennium Development Goals.
- National and local policies and legislation reviewed and revised, eliminating bottlenecks and ensuring strong and consistent incentives for local sustainable development.
- Local arid national capacities (human, institutional and societal) developed and contributing to sustainable development, including poverty alleviation, in their communities.
- Networks formed, supporting civic engagement and responsible local leadership. Information and communications systems in place, helping communities participate in decisions governing their involvement in the global economy.
- Broad participatory platforms established, designing, implementing and monitoring strategies, plans and other planning instruments
- Resource mobilisation campaigns activated, assisting communities to overcome marginalisation and other barriers to competing successfully in a globalising world.
- Functional partnerships and networks involving communities with national, regional and international partners created, supporting local capacity development for sustainable development that includes poverty reduction.

Further details at **www.undp.org**

---

2. Regional-Governmental: Global Compact

The Global Compact is a UN-sponsored platform for 'encouraging and promoting good corporate practices and learning experiences in the areas of human rights, labour and the environment'. Like the UNDP's focus on sustainable development, it is another prime example of the language of human rights entering new areas. The Global Compact is relevant for its links to development and equity in the world of international trade.

Initiated in Davos in 1999 by UN Secretary-General Kofi Annan, the Global Compact is underpinned by three key documents: the Universal Declaration of Human Rights; the Fundamental Principles and Rights at Work of the International Labour Organisation; and the Earth Summit – Agenda 21 principles on the environment. According to the official line 'These three texts express a clear set of universal values supported by all governments' and point out that 'no other initiative on corporate social responsibility has such universal and legitimate underpinning'.

The Global Compact is important as a starting point for potential partnerships and value-based linkages between business and UN. It is the opportunity for business, in a sense, to show its alignment with the principles set down in international treaties and in support of the goals of the United Nations. As such it represents 'a basis for structured dialogue between the UN, business, labour and civil society on improving corporate practices in the social arena. Finally, the Compact offers a means to significantly broaden the number of companies undertaking such activities'. Aware of the popular resentment – or at least the demonstrable anger of many human rights and anti-globalisation protestors – of multinational companies since the world trade talks at Seattle, the Global Compact is seen as a way of maintaining dialogue while retaining open world markets.

The nature and definition of the commitment to the Global Compact (in 2003) is defined in simple, practical terms, committing business to:

1. Issue a clear statement of support for the Global Compact and its principles, and engage in public advocacy for the Compact.
2. Post once a year on the Global Compact website: (**www.unglobalcompact.org**) a concrete example of progress made or lessons learned in implementing the principles. This can take many forms, e.g. changes in internal management policies or concrete operational experiences.
3. Engage in partnership with UN organisations by undertaking activities that further the implementation of the principles, or by entering strategic partnerships in support of broad UN goals such as poverty eradication.

The Global Compact is not therefore 'a code of conduct; monitoring and verification of corporate practices do not fall within the mandate or the institutional capability of the United Nations':

> But neither is the Compact to be used as a corporate shield from criticism. To the contrary, it highlights the global citizenship qualities of corporations, and opens up opportunities for focused, mediated, directed and constructive dialogue.

> The Compact does not ask companies to take over the responsibilities of governments. They are asked to take action only within their respective spheres of influence. But in the case of international intergovernmental conventions which require action at the company level to be successfully implemented, for instance, corporate participation in the Global Compact can be helpful. For full details visit **www.unglobalcompact.org**

Figure 6.7 provides some links for the UNDP and related UN and other programmes relevant to the right to development.

Figure 6.7

The Right to Development: Links

United Nations Development Programme (UNDP) – New York, USA
www.undp.org

UN Human Development Report 2000: Human Rights and Human Development
www.undp.org/hdro/HDR2000

Civil Society Organisations and Participation Programme (CSOPP)
www.undp.org/csopp/CSO/index

Democratic Governance
www.magnet.undp.org

Indigenous Peoples
www.undp.org/csopp/CSO/NewFiles/ipindex

World Bank Group – Washington, USA
www.worldbank.org

Human Rights & Development
www.worldbank.org/html/extdr/rights

The Economics of Civil Wars, Crime and Violence
www.worldbank.org/research/conflict/index

World Food Programme (WFP) – Rome, Italy
www.wfp.org

United Nations University/World Institute for Development Economics Research (UNU/ WIDER)
www.wider.unu.edu

World Health Organisation (WHO) – Geneva, Switzerland
www.who.int/home-page

Emergency and humanitarian action
www.who.int/eha/disasters
Health as a bridge for peace
www.who.int/eha/trares/hbp/index

Health as a human right
www.who.int/archives/who50/en/human

3. *NGO: OXFAM*

Oxfam International is a confederation of twelve organisations working together in more than 100 countries to find lasting solutions to poverty, suffering and injustice. Because many of the causes of poverty are global in nature, members of Oxfam International believe they can achieve greater impact in addressing issues of poverty by their collective efforts. To achieve the maximum impact on poverty, Oxfam link up their work on development programs, humanitarian response, lobbying for policy changes at national and global level: 'Our popular campaigns and communications work is aimed at mobilizing public opinion for change.' (Oxfam, 2002, visit **www.oxfam.org.uk**) Figures 6.8 and 6.9 provide some statements of basic principles for the organisation.

Figure 6.8

Oxfam Sound Bites

We work with poor people
We seek to help people organize so that they might gain better access to the opportunities they need to improve their livelihoods and govern their own lives. We also work with people affected by humanitarian disasters, with preventive measures, preparedness, as well as emergency relief.

We influence powerful people
Experience of the real issues confronting poor people is linked to high-level research and lobbying aiming to change international policies and practices in ways which would ensure that poor people have the rights, opportunities and resources they need to improve and control their lives.

We join hands with all people
Popular campaigning, alliance building and media work designed to raise awareness among the public of the real solutions to global poverty, to enable and motivate people to play an active part in the movement for change, and to foster a sense of global citizenship.

Further details at **www.oxfam.org.uk**

Figure 6.9

Oxfam and Development: A Rights Based Approach

Oxfam takes a rights-based approach to development, believing that poverty is a state of powerlessness in which people are unable to exercise their basic rights. We work on the principle that all people enjoy certain rights. This provides not only a moral basis for our work, but also a legal one. Many rights are enshrined in international agreements, covenants and declarations signed on to by the great majority of the world's governments at international summits and conferences.

• The right to a sustainable livelihood – basic needs such as food, shelter and clean water should be achievable for all; people should be able to preserve the natural resources on which they depend.
• The right to services – health, education and other services should be available to all.

- The right to life and security – people should live free from fear or displacement due to wars, crime and other violence.
- The right to be heard – people should be able to organize, speak out and take part in decisions which affect them.
- The right to an identity – people should live free from discrimination on the grounds of gender, ethnicity or other issues of identity.

Oxfam International plans its work around a series of Strategic Change Objectives which set targets for concrete changes in the achievement of the rights listed above.

Further details at **www.oxfam.org.uk**

References, Further Reading and Research

Bendell, Jem (ed) (2000) *Terms for Endearment: Business, NGOs and Sustainable Development* (Sheffield: Greenleaf)

Brown, Lester R. (2001) *State of the World 2001: Progress Towards a Sustainable Society* (London: Earthscan)

Carisnaes, Walter, Thomas Risse and Beth A. Simmons (eds) (2002) *Handbook of International Relations* (London: SAGE)

Confederation of British Industry (2001) *The CBI Environmental Management Handbook: Challenges for Business* (London: Earthscan)

Department for International Development (2000) *Halving World Poverty by 2015* (London: DFID)

Hamel, Pierre (ed) (2001) *Globalisation and Social Movements* (Basingstoke: Palgrave)

Keekok, Lee, Alan Holland and Desmond McNeill (eds) (2000) *Global Sustainable Development in the Twenty-First Century* (Edinburgh: Edinburgh University Press)

Kliot, Nurit and David Newman (eds) *Geopolitics at the End of the Twentieth Century* (London: Frank Cass)

Organisation for Economic Co-operation and Development (2000) *The Creative Society of the 21st Century* (Paris: OECD)

Reed, Charles (ed) (2001) *Development Matters: Christian Perspectives on Globalisation* (London: Church House Publishing)

Roddick, Anita (2001) *Take It Personally: How Globalisation Affects You and How to Fight Back* (London: Thorsons)

Schechter, Michael G. (2001) *United Nations-Sponsored World Conferences: Focus on Impact and Follow-Up* (Tokyo: United Nations University Press)

Went, Robert (20000 *Globalisation: Neoliberal Challenge, Radical Response* (Sterling, Virginia: Pluto)

CHAPTER SEVEN

Freedom of Expression and Censorship

Everyone has the right to freedom of opinion and expression; this right includes freedom to hold opinions without interference and to seek, receive and impart information and ideas through any media and regardless of frontiers.
Article 19, Universal Declaration of Human Rights

Figure 7.1

Freedom of Expression: Chapter Headings

Background Notes: Defining Freedom of Expression

Rights to freedom of expression have the potential to be flaunted in contexts as diverse as print journalism, film, television, media, Internet, radio, visual arts, theatre, literature. Work can be censored or banned and authors persecuted, imprisoned and murdered for political, religious, sexual or other reasons. The accessible *100 Banned Books* (Karolides, Bald and Sova, 1999) illustrates this aptly, showing that texts from novels to political treatises and sacred scripture like the Bible and the Qur'an have all been restricted over the centuries. Restriction of freedom of expression is far from an historical matter. Media and journalistic work is more restricted the world over than one might imagine, and professional organisations exist to campaign against and combat such restrictions. The BBC, for instance, has been banned from reporting directly from Zimbabwe since 2001, apart from during the Cricket World Cup of 2003.

One of the most recent issues has been about freedom of expression on the Internet: debates about and prosecutions over pornography; the right to privacy of communication are just two issues that regularly surface in the media. Freedom of expression, like freedom of religion and belief, is not only amongst the most sensitive of rights and the most contested but is also the least easy to resolve. What may be freedom of expression to one individual or socio-cultural group may well (and frequently does) cause offence to other individuals or groups.

The most high profile *literary* case in the late twentieth century was the Salman Rushdie case. A *fatwah*, originating from the Islamic state of Iran, was issued against the British author for his novel, *Satanic Verses*. There has been much in the post-September 11 world about the clash of universal human rights and certain religious traditions, Huntington's Clash of Civilisations debate has resurfaced. This is a worthy reminder that clashes between religious, value and fundamental rights to freedom of expression can also surface within liberal, western democracies supposedly founded upon the principles of basic rights and freedoms. J. K. Rowling's Harry Potter novels, for instance, are amongst the most censored of any modern work, with bans applied, largely by Christian fundamentalists, in Australia, Canada, England, Germany, but especially in the United States of America.

International Legal Standards: Defending Freedom of Expression

International legal standards focusing on or of relevance to freedom of expression are outlined in Figure 7.2. At times of tyranny and oppression, the writer, the artist, the film-maker and the musician can all provide a powerful focus for resistance. Oppressive regimes ensure that such forms of artistic expression, along with all aspects of the media, are controlled. The Index on Censorship has called this work the 'embarrassment of tyrannies' (Webb and Bell, 1997). Far from being a luxury, freedom of artistic and journalistic expression are foundational to democracies, and anathema to dictatorships.

Figure 7.2

International Legal Standards: Defending Freedom of Expression

Convention on the International Right of Correction (16 December 1952, into effect 24 August 1962)

Covenant on Civil and Political Rights (1966)

International Covenant on Social, Economic and Cultural Rights (1966)

Declaration of the Principles of International Cultural Co-operation (UNESCO) (4 November 1966)

Recommendation concerning Education for International Understanding, Co-operation and Peace and Education relating to Human Rights and Fundamental Freedoms (UNESCO) (19 November 1974)

For full texts of the documents, follow links at **www.unhchr.org**

Featured Document: Convention on the International Right of Correction (1952)

The preamble of the Convention on the International Right of Correction begins with the statement that the Contracting States desire 'to implement the right of their peoples to be fully and reliably informed' and 'to improve understanding between their peoples through the free flow of information and opinion'. The post-World War Two context is immediately evident with the rejoinder that this will thereby protect humankind 'from the scourge of war, to prevent the recurrence of aggression from any source, and to combat all propaganda which is either designed or likely to provoke or encourage any threat to peace, breach of the peace, or act of aggression'.

False reporting and propaganda are seen as potential dangers in peace as well as war, the publication of inaccurate reports a 'danger to the maintenance of friendly relations between peoples and to the preservation of peace'. Created in a world before mass television, global media and Internet, the principal targets for the Convention are radio and print journalism, especially in the context of States that do not 'provide for a right of correction of which foreign governments may avail themselves' and the desirability 'to institute such a right on the international level'.

Figure 7.3

Convention on the International Right of Correction
16 December 1952 entry into force 24 August 1962

Article 1 presents definitions of the terms of the Convention:
'1. "News dispatch" means news material transmitted in writing or by means of telecommunications, in the form customarily employed by information agencies in transmitting such news material, before publication, to newspapers, news periodicals and broadcasting organisations.

2. "Information agency" means a press, broadcasting, film, television or facsimile organisation, public or private, regularly engaged in the collection and dissemination of news material, created and organized under the laws and regulations of the Contracting State in which the central organisation is domiciled and which, in each Contracting State where it operates, functions under the laws and regulations of that State.

3. "Correspondent" means a national of a Contracting State or an individual employed by an information agency of a Contracting State, who in either case is regularly engaged in the collection and the reporting of news material, and who when outside his State is identified as a correspondent by a valid passport or by a similar document internationally acceptable.'

Article 2 provides an overview of 'the professional responsibility of correspondents and information agencies' to report facts 'without discrimination and in their proper context and thereby to promote respect for human rights and fundamental freedoms, to further international understanding and co-operation and to contribute to the maintenance of international peace and security'. It also states that 'all correspondents and information agencies should, in the case of news dispatches transmitted or published by them and which have been demonstrated to be false or distorted, follow the customary practice of transmitting through the same channels, or of publishing corrections of such dispatches'. Its concern is with news dispatches 'capable of injuring its relations with other States or its national prestige or dignity transmitted from one country to another by correspondents or information agencies' where such is 'published or disseminated abroad is false or distorted'. In such cases, the offended party 'may submit its version of the facts' – defined in the Convention as a 'communique' – to 'the Contracting States within whose territories such dispatch has been published or disseminated. A copy of the communique shall be forwarded at the same time to the correspondent or information agency concerned to enable that correspondent or information agency to correct the news dispatch in question.' Such communiques 'may be issued only with respect to news dispatches and must be without comment or expression of opinion' and no longer 'than is necessary to correct the alleged inaccuracy or distortion'.

Article 3 states that 'with the least possible delay and in any case not later than five clear days from the date of receiving a communique' a State, 'whatever its opinion concerning the facts in question', shall:

'(a) Release the communique to the correspondents and information agencies operating in its territory through the channels customarily used for the release of news concerning international affairs for publications; and
(b) Transmit the communique to the headquarters of the information agency whose correspondent was responsible for originating the dispatch in question, if such headquarters are within its territory.

2. In the event that a Contracting State does not discharge its obligation under this article, with respect to the communique of another Contracting State, the latter may accord, on the basis of reciprocity, similar treatment to a communique thereafter submitted to it by the defaulting State.'

Article 4 states that if any of the Contracting States to which a communique has been transmitted fails to fulfil the set obligations laid down, redress may be made to the Secretary-General of the United Nations.

Article 5 states that 'Any dispute between any two or more Contracting States concerning the interpretation or application of the present Convention which is not settled by negotiations shall be referred to the International Court of Justice for decision unless the Contracting States agree to another mode of settlement.'

Articles 6–14 contain reference to administrative detail on the process of signing (**Article 6**) ratification (**Articles 7** and **8**), the extent of the provisions of the Convention (**Article 9**), denunciation (**Article 10**), when the Convention will cease to be in force (**Article 11**), requests for revision (**Article 12**), responsibilities of the Secretary-General in terms of notification (**Article 13**), the translations and deposition of the Convention (**Article 14**).

For a full text of the document, follow links at **www.unhchr.org**

Organisations Concerned with Freedom of Expression: UN/Regional-Governmental, NGO

1. UN/Regional-Governmental: United Nations Educational, Scientific and Cultural Organisation UNESCO

The United Nations Educational, Scientific and Cultural Organisation (UNESCO) – based in Paris (**www.unesco.org**) – was formed in the post-War period to cater for the immediate social and cultural needs of those worst affected by the global conflict. As with many other organisations formed at the time, its scope and range of activity rapidly expanded.

Technically a key organ of the United Nations machinery, it has a strong national and regional focus with many offices based in and named after the constituent countries, for example UNESCO UK. Today UNESCO defines its 'forms of action' across the following wide spectrum as:

- Establishment of international standards: conventions, agreements, recommendations
- Declarations
- Conferences and meetings
- Studies and research
- Publications: books, periodicals, reports and documents
- Technical and advisory services to Member States: staff missions, consultants, supplies and equipment
- Training courses, seminars and workshops
- Subventions to NGOs
- Financial contributions; fellowships, study grants and travel grants

The list of selected national and regional programmes and projects since 1945 (many of which are ongoing) present an idea of what this has meant over the past five decades of its operation:

- Reconstruction and rehabilitation programme 1945–1950
- UNESCO Translation Programme – representative works of world literature: African, Creole, European, Latin American, Oceanian and Oriental series
- 1948 – UNESCO Fellowship Programme
- 1948 – Education of Palestine refugees
- 1948 – UNESCO Coupons Programme (UNESCO coupons overcome foreign exchange difficulties in buying books and other cultural materials)
- 1955 – Participation Programme
- 1957–1962 Major Project on Scientific Research on Arid Lands 1957–1962
- 1957–1966 Major Project on Mutual Appreciation of Eastern and Western Cultural Values
- 1959–1965 Major Project of Education in Latin America and the Caribbean
- 1960–1980 International Campaign to save the monuments of Nubia
- 1961 – Oceanographic research and coastal zone management
- 1966–1975 World Experimental Literacy Programme (WELP)
- 1980 – International Programme for the Development of Communication (IPDC)
- 1984 – Education for All
- 1988 – Integral Study of the Silk Roads: Roads of Dialogue 1988–
- 1989 – Priority Africa
- 1994 – Culture of Peace Programme
- 1996–2005 – World Solar Programme

Some recent regional development projects include:

- 1980 – Population Education in Secondary Schools, China
- 1981 – Pan African News Agency
- 1987 – Support for the National System of Curriculum Improvement and Adaptation, Guatemala
- 1988 – Revival of the Library of Alexandria, Egypt (EGY/88/003)
- 1996 – Pilot projects for the education of street children (Namibia, Guinea, Mali, Togo, Brazil, Russia, Romania)

A list of major UNESCO conferences of the 1990s demonstrates UNESCO's commitment to scientific research and education at all levels:

1990 World Conference of Education for All, Jomtien, Thailand (with UNDP, UNICEF and the World Bank)
1995 Audience Africa, Paris
1996 World Solar Summit, Harare
1998 World Conference on Higher Education, Paris
1999 World Science Conference, Budapest
2000 World Education Forum, Dakar

Figure 7.4 provides a list of some of UNESCO's important publications.

Figure 7.4

UNESCO Publications

Since 1946, UNESCO has published more 10,000 titles across the full range of its activities, including book length reports, scholarly research and newsletters.

Recent books – selected titles:
General History of Africa I–VIII (1981–1999)
World Communication Report, 1989 (1997; in 1999 as World Communication and Information Report 1999–2000)
World Education Report (1991, 1993, 1995, 1998, 2000)
History of Civilisations of Central Asia I–VI, (1992–)
World Science Report, (1993, 1996,1998)
Learning: The Treasure Within (1996) (Delors Commission report)
Our Cultural Diversity (1998) (Perez de Cuellar Commission report)
World Culture Report (1998, 2000)
World Social Science Report (1999)

Main (current) periodicals of UNESCO:
1948 – *The UNESCO Courier* 1948– (illustrated monthly, published in 27 languages and in Braille)
1948 – [*Museum*, 1948–1992 (now, since 1993–)] *Museum International*
1949 – *International Social Science Journal* (ISSJ)
1965 – *Nature and resources*
1969 – *Prospects: quarterly review of education*

1950 – *Archivum: international review on archives*. International Council on Archives

1955 – *Diogenes: an international review of philosophy and humanistic studies*. International Council for Philosophy and Humanistic Studies

1955 – *International Review of Education*. UNESCO Institute for Education, Hamburg

News bulletins:

- 1946 *UNESCO Bulletin 1946*
- 1947 *UNESCO Monitor 1947*
- 1948–1955 *UNESCO Official Bulletin*
- 1949–1955 *UNESCO Newsletter*
- 1955–1980 *Chronicle*
- 1979–1987 *UNESCO News*
- 1988 – *UNESCO Sources*

See also:

- UNESDOC database on the Internet. Full text of all official UNESCO documents since the end of 1995
- UNESBIB database of more than 100,000 bibliographical references to UNESCO documents, publications and the library collection.

www.unesco.org

The immense scope and range of UNESCO's work is illustrated also by the links the organisation has to many aspects of human rights – from education through to working for democracy and pluralism, as illustrated in Figure 7.5.

Figure 7.5

UNESCO Links

United Nations Educational, Scientific and Cultural Organisation (UNESCO) – Paris
www.unesco.org

Division of Human Rights, Democracy, Peace and Tolerance
www.unesco.org/human_rights/index

Management of Social Transformations
Programme (MOST):
www.unesco.org/most

Multiculturalism
www.unesco.org/most/most1

Linguistic rights
www.unesco.org/most/ln1

Religious rights
www.unesco.org/most/rr1

Cultural heritage
www.unesco.org/culture/heritage

Intercultural dialogue and pluralism
www.unesco.org/culture/dial

World Intellectual Property Organisation (WIPO) – Geneva, Switzerland
www.wipo.int

Traditional Knowledge
www.wipo.org/traditionalknowledge/introduction/index

Universal Declaration on Linguistic Rights
www.troc.es/ciemen/mercator

Child Rights
www.unicef.org/crc/index

The State of the World's Children 2000
www.unicef.org/sowc00/uwar2

World Education Forum: Dakar 2000
www.unicef.org/efa/results

---

2. NGO: International PEN (Poets, Essayists, Novelists)

International PEN (Poets, Essayists, Novelists) rightly describes itself as a 'worldwide association of writers'. The organisation has three guiding principles:

- To promote intellectual cooperation and understanding among writers
- To create a world community of writers that would emphasises the central role of literature in the development of world culture
- To defend literature against the many threats to its survival that the modern world poses.

It has a highly prestigious list of literary Nobel laureates amongst it members. Presidents of PEN have included Alberto Moravia, Heinrich Böll, Arthur Miller, Pierre Emmanuel, Mario Vargas Llosa and György Konrád. Existing 'to promote friendship and intellectual co-operation among writers everywhere, regardless of their political or other views' and 'to fight for freedom of expression and to defend vigorously writers suffering from oppressive regimes' PEN's history is an illustrious one. It was founded in London in 1921 by Mrs C. A. Dawson Scott, its first president being John Galsworthy. Early members included Joseph Conrad, George Bernard Shaw and H. G. Wells.

As a premier NGO concerned with freedom of expression and literary freedoms worldwide, PEN has representative, consultative status at UNESCO. With many centres around the world, membership 'is open to all qualified writers, regardless of nationality, language, race, colour or religion, and every member is required to sign the PEN Charter'. The PEN Charter is based on resolutions passed at its International Congresses and may be summarized as follows:

PEN affirms that:

1. Literature, national though it be in origin, knows no frontiers, and should remain common currency between nations in spite of political or international upheavals.

2. In all circumstances, and particularly in time of war, works of art, the patrimony of humanity at large, should be left untouched by national or political passion.

3. Members of PEN should at all times use what influence they have in favour of good understanding and mutual respect between nations; they pledge themselves to do their utmost to dispel race, class and national hatreds, and to champion the ideal of one humanity living in peace in one world.

4. PEN stands for the principle of unhampered transmission of thought within each nation and between all nations, and members pledge themselves to oppose any form of suppression of freedom of expression in the country and community to which they belong, as well as throughout the world wherever this is possible. PEN declares for a free press and opposes arbitrary censorship in time of peace. It believes that the necessary advance of the world towards a more highly organized political and economic order renders a free criticism of governments, administrations and institutions imperative. And since freedom implies voluntary restraint, members pledge themselves to oppose such evils of a free press as mendacious publication, deliberate falsehood and distortion of facts for political and personal ends.

Membership of PEN is open to all qualified writers, editors and translators who subscribe to these aims, without regard to nationality, language, race, colour or religion.

The activities of International PEN are subdivided into various project areas, each with a specific operational focus but all linked to a common commitment to the International PEN Charter. The three areas are:

Writers in Prison
The Writers in Prison Committee of International PEN, 'works on behalf of persecuted writers worldwide'. It was established in 1960 'in response to increasing attempts to silence voices of dissent by imprisoning writers and 'currently monitors the cases of almost 900 writers annually, including writers imprisoned, tortured, threatened, attacked, disappeared and killed for the peaceful practice of their profession, and lobbies on their behalf'. A distinguishing feature of the Writers in Prison Committee 'among other human rights organisations is its commitment to long-term case-work' which may extend over a period of many years.

The Writers in Prison Committee maintains a regularly updated database of all cases of abuses against writers and journalists, with a case list produced in printed form twice a year, and information on individual cases or specific countries available on request from the Writers in Prison Committee headquarters in London. The Writers in Prison Committee produces a bi-monthly newsletter, Centre to Centre.

Writers for Peace
The Writers for Peace Committee was founded in 1984, at the height of the Cold War by a Slovene, Milos Milkeln. Annual meetings organized by the Slovene Centre at Lake Bled 'discuss their actions regarding armed conflicts in different regions of the world' The Committee aims 'to organize dialogues and peaceful coexistence between writers and intellectuals in different regions of conflict, with activities including 'writing protest letters to presidents of

countries that are involved in armed conflicts or practise repression of human rights and free-dom of expression'. In particular, the Writers for Peace Committee focuses 'on the abuse of literary language for the purpose of war propaganda and the instigation of hatred against nationalities, religions, cultures, etc., (so-called hate speech)'.

Exiled Writers

The Writers in Exile Network is the most recent of International PEN projects, formed in Moscow in 2000. The network 'works on behalf of writers who have been forced into exile. It provides personal and professional information and guidance to help writers integrate into a safe country'. It was established 'to share and exchange information and experiences, and to raise awareness both locally and internationally about the problems facing exiled writers'. Based on the premise that 'writers from other countries enrich and invigorate the cultures that take them in' the Writers in Exile Network was 'formed in response to the growing number of writers fleeing persecution'. Figure 7.6 illustrates the global, on-the-ground reach of International PEN.

Figure 7.6

Selected International PEN World Wide Links

Australia
www.plateupress.com.au
www.perthpen.virtual.com.au
www.pen.org.au
Austria
www.penclub.at
Canada
www.pen.canada.ca
Denmark
www.pen.dk
England
www.pen.org.uk
Iran (in exile)
www.iran-pen.com
Japan
www.mmjp.or.jp/japan-penclub
Macedonia
www.pen.org.mk
Montenegro
www.montenegro.org/pen
New Zealand
www.arachna.co.nz/nzsa
Poland
www.penclub.atomnet.pl
Russia
www.penrussia.org

Sardinia
www.uniss.it/fch/pen/index
Scotland
www.scottishpen.org
Sweden
www.pensweden.org
Switzerland and Italy
www.writers-prison.org
USA
www.pen.org
www.pen.usa-west.org

Other Links
Index on Censorship **www.index.org**

Charter '88 **www.charter88.org**

Human Rights Watch **www.hrw.org**

Links to the Hellman-Hammett Awards and through world reports to 'Freedom of Expression on the Internet'

Global Internet Liberty Campaign (GILC) **www.gilc.org**

Council of Europe Cybercrime Treaty
www.conventions.coe.int/Treaty/EN/projets/FinalCybercrime

Oxford Internet Institute
www.ox.oii

References, Research and Further Reading

American Library Association (2002) *Intellectual Freedom Manual* (Washington: Office for Intellectual Freedom of the American Library Association)

Barker, Martin, Jane Arthurs and Ramaswami Harindranath *The Crash Controversy: Censorship Campaigns and Film Reception* (London: Wallflower Press)

Bedford, Carmel (2000) *Fiction, Fact and Fatwa: The Rushdie Defence Campaign* (London: Article 19)

de Baets, Antoon (2002) *Censorship of Historical Thought: A World Guide, 1945–2000* (Westport and London: Greenwood Press)

Dollimore, Jonathan (2001) *Sex, Literature and Censorship* (Cambridge: Polity Press)

Goldstein, Robert Justin (ed) (2001) *Political Censorship* (London: Fitzroy Dearborn)

Jones, Derek (2001) *Censorship: A World Encyclopedia* (London: Dearborn)

Karolides, Nicholas J., Margaret Bald and Dawn B. Sova (eds) (1999) *100 Banned Books: Censorship Histories of World Literature* (New York: Checkmark Books)

Kolbert, Kathryn and Zak Mettger (eds) *Censoring the Web* (New York: New Press)

Liberty (1999) *Liberating Cyberspace: Civil Liberties, Human Rights and the Internet* (London: Pluto)

Mills, Jane (ed) (2001) *The Money Shot: Cinema, Sin and Censorship* (Annandale: Pluto Press Australia)

Mostyn, Trevor (1999) *Censorship in Islamic Societies* (London: Saqi)

Saunders, Stonor Frances (2000) *Who Paid the Piper?: The CIA and the Cultural Cold War* (New York: New Press)

Simmons, John S. and Eliza T. Desang (2001) *School Censorship in the 21st Century: A Guide for Teachers and School Library Media Specialists* (Newark: International Reading Association)

Steele, Philip (2000) *Freedom of Speech* (London: Watts)

UN (2002) *The Committee on Economic, Social and Cultural Rights* (New York: United Nations)

Webb, W.L. and Rose Bell (1997) *An Embarrassment of Tyrannies: Twenty-Five Years of Index on Censorship* (London: Victor Gollancz)

CHAPTER EIGHT

Freedom of Religion and Belief

Everyone has the right to freedom of thought, conscience and religion.
Article 18, Universal Declaration of Human Rights

Figure 8.1

Freedom of Religion and Belief: Chapter Headings

Background Notes: Defining Freedom of Religion and Belief

Religion has always had political consequences. In the era of the United Nations, traditional religious beliefs have in some cases blended harmoniously and in others clashed violently with notions of universal human rights (Gearon 2002). It was Huntington (1992) who revitalised for the 1990s the ancient notion of a 'clash of civilisations', and Fukuyama (1992) with his 'end of history' thesis, who suggested that western, liberal democracy based on universal human rights had won the contest in this clash.

Haynes's work (1998) builds on Casanova's (1994) seminal challenge to the largely unchallenged secularisation thesis, that in modern societies religion becomes less and less relevant. A major authority on the role of religion in global politics, Haynes presents a useful summary of the power struggle between Islam and Christianity:

> Contemporaneous with the end of Islam as a cultural force in Western Europe was the beginning of the expansion of European influence across the globe. The search for gold in the Americas led in the early sixteenth century to the formation of European colonies there, and colonies were also established in the Caribbean and Asia. Between the fifteenth and nineteenth centuries, the spread of Christianity to Africa, accompanied by the extraction of millions of slaves, and to the Middle East and the Americas added to the emerging web of global interactions. Despite this global expansion of Christian Europeans, the social and cultural systems defined by Islam survived across Eurasia and the worldwide influence of Islamic beliefs persisted. (Haynes 1998; cited Gearon, 2002: 17–30)

Haynes argues that 'in the early years of the twentieth century, communism and fascism appeared as universal, secular ideologies with the propensity to attract converts across state boundaries. There was a process of global ideological differentiation, deepening after the Second World War, when the defeat of fascism led to the emergence of liberal democracy as the dominant but not yet global ideology.' Throughout the Cold War 'one set of ideas – communism – was pitched against another – liberal democracy and its economic counterpart, capitalism – in a struggle for dominance that culminated in the defeat of Soviet-style communism at the end of the 1980s.'

Yet the end of the Cold War has produced a 'new agenda' for international relations that includes 'the environment, illegal drugs, AIDS, terrorism, migration, refugees, human rights, new conceptions of security, democratisation and religious actors with political goals'. As Haynes comments, 'Most of these issues are linked to cultural behaviour but they are also associated with religion as an aspect of cultural behaviour'. Interestingly, Haynes posited a thesis in the late 1990s that there are two perceived religious and or cultural threats to western style democracy based on universal human rights: Confucianism and the so called 'Asian values' debate on the one hand and on the other, as he has so ably set out in historical context, Islam. His conclusions suggest that neither is the threat that they are perceived to be. But then even after the Gulf War (1990–1) when many commentators perceived Islamic fundamentalism to be a threat to any new post-Cold War world order, no one expected the events of September 11.

International Legal Standards: Defending Freedom of Religion and Belief

Since the formation of the United Nations, human rights issues related to religion and belief have been the focus of several international instruments:

• The Universal Declaration of Human Rights (1948)
• The Arcot Krishnaswami Study (1959)
• The International Covenant on Civil and Political Rights (1966)
• The International Covenant on Social, Economic and Cultural Rights (1966)
• The Declaration on the Elimination of All Forms of Intolerance and
• Discrimination Based on Religion or Belief (1981)

A list of these and related international standards is shown in Figure 8.2. One of the academic authorities on these is Lerner (2000).

Recently, issues of religion have increasingly come to the fore in a United Nations formally cautious about being explicit about arguably the most contentious of all human rights. While a post-September 11 context has further highlighted the issue of potential conflict in worldview, the issue of this fissure between universal rights promulgated by the United Nations and its machinery and particular cultural, especially religious, traditions has been a live one for many years (Ayton-Shenker, 1995). The cruel historical irony should not be lost that the World Conference Against Racism, Xenophobia and Other Forms of Discrimination in Durban, South Africa (September 2001) concluded its business on an optimistic note according to one major human rights organisation just the day before September 11 (HRW, 2001).

The Universal Declaration of Human Rights includes a number of articles of relevance to freedom of religion and belief. These include Article 2 (forbidding prejudicial distinctions of any kind, including those related to religion), Article 26 (on the rights to a particular religious education) and Article 29 (on responsibilities and proscription against limitations of proclaimed rights). The foundation stone of freedom of religion and belief, though, is to be found in Article 18 of the Universal Declaration of Human Rights. This states that, 'Everyone has the right to freedom of: thought, conscience and religion; this right includes freedom to change his religion or belief, and freedom, either alone or in community with others and in public or private, to manifest his religion or belief in teaching, practice, worship and observance.'

As Lerner (2000) comments, 'Article 18 greatly influenced the texts incorporated in the 1966 Covenants, and was influential in regional treaties and the 1981 Declaration, divided Article 18 into two parts, the first clause guarantees the right to freedom of thought, conscience, and religion; the second enumerates the specific rights included therein. This second part is not exhaustive. It only contains those rights that the United Nations thought essential to include because their observance might not be universal at present.'

Figure 8.2

International Legal Standard: Defending Freedom of Religion and Belief

Declaration on the Elimination of All Forms of Intolerance and of Discrimination based on Religion or Belief (25 November 1981)
Declaration on the Rights of Persons Belonging to National or Ethnic, Religious and Linguistic Minorities (18 December 1992)
Oslo Declaration on Freedom of Religion and Belief (1998)
World Conference against Racism, Xenophobia and Related Forms of Discrimination (September, 2002)

For a full text of the document, follow links at **www.unhchr.org**

Featured Document: Declaration on the Elimination of All Forms of Intolerance and of Discrimination Based on Religion or Belief (1981)

The preamble to the UN Declaration on the Elimination of All Forms of Intolerance and Discrimination Based on Religion or Belief (1981) restates the wider context of Charter of the UN. Notably this reiterates the 'dignity and equality inherent in all human beings', international commitment on the promotion of universal human rights and fundamental freedoms for all, 'without distinction as to race, sex, language or religion' and the principles of non-discrimination and equality before the law and the right to freedom of thought, conscience, religion and belief'.

As with the Convention on the International Rights of Correction, UN Declaration on the Elimination of All Forms of Intolerance and Discrimination Based on Religion or Belief also emphasises the role of such freedoms in the maintenance of a stable international order: 'Considering that the disregard and infringement of human rights and fundamental freedoms, in particular of the right to freedom of thought, conscience, religion or whatever belief, have brought, directly or indirectly, wars and great suffering to mankind, especially where they serve as a means of foreign interference in the internal affairs of other States and amount to kindling hatred between peoples and nations.' Positively phrased, 'freedom of religion and belief should also contribute to the attainment of the goals of world peace, social justice and friendship among peoples and to the elimination of ideologies or practices of colonialism and racial discrimination'.

Yet it is not simply past ills that are the concern of the UN, for the 1981 Declaration is also concerned about 'manifestations of intolerance and by the existence of discrimination in matters of religion or belief still in evidence in some areas of the world'. The 1981 Declaration, summarised in Figure 8.3, also offers a commitment to adopt 'all necessary measures for the speedy elimination of such intolerance in all its forms and manifestations and to prevent and combat discrimination on the ground of religion or belief'. The range of atrocity and genocide over the following two decades (especially in the former Yugoslavia and in Rwanda) would seem indicative of a massive failure by the UN system.

Figure 8.3

Declaration on the Elimination of All Forms of Intolerance and of Discrimination Based on Religion or Belief
25 November 1981

Article 1 states that 'Everyone shall have the right to freedom of thought, conscience and religion. This right shall include freedom to have a religion or whatever belief of his choice, and freedom, either individually or in community with others and in public or private, to manifest his religion or belief in worship, observance, practice and teaching.' Further, no one shall be subject to coercion that would impair their freedom to have a religion or belief of their choice. Here, 'Freedom to manifest one's religion or belief may be subject only to such limitations as are prescribed by law and are necessary to protect public safety, order, health or morals or the fundamental rights and freedoms of others.'

Article 2 states that 'No one shall be subject to discrimination by any State, institution, group of persons, or person on the grounds of religion or other belief. For the purposes of the Declaration, intolerance and discrimination based on religion or belief means 'any distinction, exclusion, restriction or preference based on religion or belief and having as its purpose or as its effect nullification or impairment of the recognition, enjoyment or exercise of human rights and fundamental freedoms on an equal basis.'

Article 3 states that 'Discrimination between human beings on the grounds of religion or belief constitutes an affront to human dignity and a disavowal of the principles of the Charter of the United Nations, and shall be condemned as a violation of the human rights and fundamental freedoms proclaimed in the Universal Declaration of Human Rights'. Such may be regarded as 'an obstacle to friendly and peaceful relations between nations'.

Article 4 sets forth the responsibilities of States to 'take effective measures to prevent and eliminate discrimination on the grounds of religion or belief in the recognition, exercise and enjoyment of human rights and fundamental freedoms in all fields of civil, economic, political, social and cultural life'.

Article 5 states that 'The parents or, as the case may be, the legal guardians of the child have the right to organize the life within the family in accordance with their religion or belief and bearing in mind the moral education in which they believe the child should be brought up.' Article 5 also contains reference to the rights of the child to have 'access to education in the matter of religion or belief' according to the wishes of parents or guardians.

Article 6 outlines in more detail what is meant by 'the right to freedom of thought, conscience, religion or belief', including the following freedoms:

'(a) To worship or assemble in connection with a religion or belief, and to establish and maintain places for these purposes

(b) To establish and maintain appropriate charitable or humanitarian institutions

(c) To make, acquire and use to an adequate extent the necessary articles and materials related to the rites or customs of a religion or belief

(d) To write, issue and disseminate relevant publications in these areas

(e) To teach a religion or belief in places suitable for these purposes

(f) To solicit and receive voluntary financial and other contributions from individuals and institutions

(g) To train, appoint, elect or designate by succession appropriate leaders called for by the requirements and standards of any religion or belief

(h) To observe days of rest and to celebrate holidays and ceremonies in accordance with the precepts of one's religion or belief

(i) To establish and maintain communications with individuals and communities in matters of religion and belief at the national and international levels.'

Article 7 states that 'The rights and freedoms set forth in the present Declaration shall be accorded in national legislation in such a manner that everyone shall be able to avail himself of such rights and freedoms in practice.'

Article 8 states that 'Nothing in the present Declaration shall be construed as restricting or derogating from any right defined in the Universal Declaration of Human Rights and the International Covenants on Human Rights.'

For a full text, follow links at **www.unhchr.org**

What is important here can be summarised in three points. First, after a long neglect (or low level treatment) of religion explicitly, the UN system from the late 1970s and with the 1981

Declaration began to recognise the international significance of religion for a stable world order. Thus, during the 1990s, religion emerges explicitly in numerous international statements, gaining new and unprecedented prominence. For instance, there was the Cairo Declaration on Human Rights in Islam (1990), the Fundamental Agreement between the Holy See and the State of Israel (1993). The Vienna Declaration and Plan of Action (1993) and the follow-up to the World Conference on Human Rights UN High Commissioner on Human Rights (1998) also gave some prominence to religion, important in light of their respective post-Yugoslavia and post-Rwanda contexts [especially paragraphs 34–39]. The new prominence given to religion culminated in the Oslo Declaration on Freedom of Religion and Belief (1998). Second, and indicated by both the 1981 Declaration and the 1998 Oslo Declaration, the notion of freedom of religion was itself extended to freedom of religion and belief to allow for a wider interpretation of worldviews.

Third, this has in turn had the effect of linking in a fairly direct way the fundamental first and second generation rights of 'freedom of thought, conscience and religion' to third generation rights of human solidarity, most notable in the linking of religious intolerance to the ending of racism, xenophobia and discrimination more broadly. For example, we might note the 1981 Declaration on the Elimination of All Forms of Intolerance and of Discrimination Based on Religion or Belief was followed just over a decade later by the UN Declaration on the Rights of Persons Belonging to National or Ethnic, Religious, and Linguistic Minorities (1992). Unifying religious freedom with other forms of discrimination was highlighted by the World Conference Against Racism (2001). As already noted, the conclusion of this event immediately before September 11 powerfully underlines the complexities and heightened importance of the religious dimension to universal human rights.

Organisations Concerned with Freedom of Religion and Belief: UN, Regional-Governmental and NGO

1. UN: World Conference against Racism, Racial Discrimination, Xenophobia and Related Intolerance (2002)

World Conference against Racism, Racial Discrimination, Xenophobia and Related Intolerance ended just a day or so before the attack on the Twin Towers in New York. The Conference drew on the heroic struggle of the people of South Africa against the institutionalized system of apartheid as a symbol of this wider struggle. While obviously dealing with wider issues beyond religious freedom and belief, these remained integral to the Conference's concerns. The Preamble to the Conference statement reaffirmed principles of non-discrimination, 'the principles of equality and non-discrimination in the Universal Declaration of Human Rights and encouraging respect for human rights and fundamental freedoms for all without distinction of any kind such as race, colour, sex, language, religion, political or other opinion, national or social origin, property, birth or other status'. Indirectly, the recollection that 'the United Nations Declaration on the Granting of Independence to Colonial Countries and Peoples of 1960' recalls too the memory that the imperial expansion of western empires, while motivated primarily by economic exploitation, was also justified by religious belief and evangelical fervour. Figure 8.4 presents some of the introductory comments that form the Conference's final statement, and sum up its rationale and intentions.

Figure 8.4

World Conference against Racism: General Issues

1. We declare that for the purpose of the present Declaration and Programme of Action, the victims of racism, racial discrimination, xenophobia and related intolerance are individuals or groups of individuals who are or have been negatively affected by, subjected to, or targets of these scourges.

2. We recognize that racism, racial discrimination, xenophobia and related intolerance occur on the grounds of race, colour, descent or national or ethnic origin and that victims can suffer multiple or aggravated forms of discrimination based on other related grounds such as sex, language, religion, political or other opinion, social origin, property, birth or other status.

3. We recognize and affirm that, at the outset of the third millennium, a global fight against racism, racial discrimination, xenophobia and related intolerance and all their abhorrent and evolving forms and manifestations is a matter of priority for the international community, and that this Conference offers a unique and historic opportunity for assessing and identifying all dimensions of those devastating evils of humanity with a view to their total elimination through, *inter alia*, the initiation of innovative and holistic approaches and the strengthening and enhancement of practical and effective measures at the national, regional and international levels.

4. We express our solidarity with the people of Africa in their continuing struggle against racism, racial discrimination, xenophobia and related intolerance and recognize the sacrifices made by them, as well as their efforts in raising international public awareness of these inhuman tragedies.

5. We also affirm the great importance we attach to the values of solidarity, respect, tolerance and multiculturalism, which constitute the moral ground and inspiration for our worldwide struggle against racism, racial discrimination, xenophobia and related intolerance, inhuman tragedies which have affected people throughout the world, especially in Africa, for too long.

6. We further affirm that all peoples and individuals constitute one human family, rich in diversity. They have contributed to the progress of civilisations and cultures that form the common heritage of humanity. Preservation and promotion of tolerance, pluralism and respect for diversity can produce more inclusive societies.

7. We declare that all human beings are born free, equal in dignity and rights and have the potential to contribute constructively to the development and well-being of their societies. Any doctrine of racial superiority is scientifically false, morally condemnable, socially unjust and dangerous, and must be rejected along with theories which attempt to determine the existence of separate human races.

8. We recognize that religion, spirituality and belief play a central role in the lives of millions of women and men, and in the way they live and treat other persons. Religion, spirituality and belief may and can contribute to the promotion of the inherent dignity and worth of the human person and to the eradication of racism, racial discrimination, xenophobia and related intolerance.

9. We note with concern that racism, racial discrimination, xenophobia and related intolerance may be aggravated by, *inter alia*, inequitable distribution of wealth, marginalisation and social exclusion.

10. We reaffirm that everyone is entitled to a social and international order in which all human rights can be fully realized for all, without any discrimination.

11. We note that the process of globalisation constitutes a powerful and dynamic force which should be harnessed for the benefit, development and prosperity of all countries, without exclusion. We recognize that developing countries face special difficulties in responding to this central challenge. While globalisation offers great opportunities, at present its benefits are very unevenly shared, while its costs are unevenly distributed. We thus express our determination to prevent and mitigate the negative effects of globalisation. These effects could aggravate, *inter alia*, poverty, underdevelopment, marginalisation, social exclusion, cultural homogenisation and economic disparities which may occur along racial lines, within and between States, and have an adverse impact. We further express our determination to maximize the benefits of globalisation through, *inter alia*, the strengthening and enhancement of international cooperation to increase equality of opportunities for trade, economic growth and sustainable development, global communications through the use of new technologies and increased intercultural exchange through the preservation and promotion of cultural diversity, which can contribute to the eradication of racism, racial discrimination, xenophobia and related intolerance. Only through broad and sustained efforts to create a shared future based upon our common humanity, and all its diversity, can globalisation be made fully inclusive and equitable.

12. We recognize that interregional and intraregional migration has increased as a result of globalisation, in particular from the South to the North, and stress that policies towards migration should not be based on racism, racial discrimination, xenophobia and related intolerance.

For full text and related documents, follow links at **www.un.org**

---

2. Regional-Governmental: US State Department

The 1998 International Religious Freedom Act made it a requirement for the US Secretary of State to publish an Annual Report on religious freedom worldwide. Published each September, the Annual Report on International Religious Freedom is submitted to the Committee on International Relations at the US House of Representatives and the Committee on Foreign Relations of the US Senate by the Department of State. The report is extensive and provides country-by-country accounts of religious freedoms, the infringements of and improvements in relation to such rights to belief. It is available at **www.house.gov/international_relations/** and **www.state.gov/g/drl/rls/irf/2001/** [or whichever date the Report refers]. Coverage includes the following breakdown of regions:

- Africa
- East Asia and the Pacific
- Europe and Eurasia
- Near East and North Africa

- South Asia
- Western Hemisphere

The Report contains an extremely useful executive summary – the 2001 Report was close to 700 pages.

This significant development in US State intelligence gathering in relation to religious freedom is indicative of the increasing importance attached to religious belief and its growing significance for global governance, a fact acknowledged explicitly by the Report. The US Department of State clearly links freedom of religion and the likelihood that countries that preserve this will respect other fundamental rights:

> A commitment to the inviolable and universal dignity of the human person is at the core of US human rights policy abroad, including the policy of advocating religious freedom. Governments that protect religious freedom for all their citizens are more likely to protect the other fundamental human rights. Encouraging stable, healthy democracies is a vital national interest in the United States. The spread of democracy makes for good neighbours, economic prosperity, increased trade, and a decrease in conflict. (US Department of State, 2001)

The US Department of State makes claim to draw upon two sources here: 'the history and commitment of the American people, and standards established by the international community'. These two traditions are not only 'consistent' but 'mutually supportive'.

The introduction to the Report thus speaks of the longstanding commitment of the United States to religious liberty:

> America's founders made religious freedom the first freedom of the Constitution – giving it pride of place among those liberties enumerated in the Bill of Rights – because they believed that guaranteeing the right to search for transcendent truths and ultimate human purpose was a critical component of a durable democracy. (US Department of State, 2001)

It goes on to reiterate how, in the international domain, 'Freedom of religion and conscience is one of the foundational rights in the post-War system of human rights instruments.' It again makes explicit how in 'recent years, the international commitment to religious freedom has increased'.

3. NGO: Freedom House

Freedom House is perhaps the world's foremost independent NGO concerned with issues of religious freedom. A major achievement of Freedom House has been the publication of its highly accessible *Religious Freedom in the World* (Marshall, 2000). Marshall's survey interestingly overlaps with developments in the US Department of State and its Report on International Religious Freedom, a document which Marshall welcomes but with reservations. Marshall's comment is that the US Department of State Report can lessen criticism of States that happen to be key allies at a particular time in history. Human Rights Watch similarly claim that the 'War on Terror' has lessened US Department of State criticisms of certain countries – especially in the 2001 Report where the United States required strategic allies.

The Freedom House global survey reviewed the state of religious freedom in the majority of the world's countries, providing useful snapshot insights into the political context of religious life in each. The survey criteria were developed from the UN Declaration on the Elimination of All Forms of Intolerance and of Discrimination Based on Religion or Belief, and related UN instruments. Even so, its assessment of the level of religious freedom may seem a little crude (there is a 1–7 scale, with 7 being the least tolerant and the US gaining an unambiguous 1). Nevertheless, Marshall is an astute analyst, recognising that 'surveying religious freedom is more limited than surveying human rights in general'. Interesting Marshall also makes a link but differentiates freedom of religion with freedom of expression, arguing that it is also 'different from surveying particular human rights, such as press freedom, which focus only on particular organisations or practices':

> With freedom of the press, one can look at the intensity of controls on particular media and the weight of penalties applied with those controls. But, unlike press freedom, religious freedom cannot be focused on the freedoms of certain organisations and individuals. Religious freedom cuts across a wide range of human rights. (Freedom House, 2002, visit **www.freedomhouse.org**)

Marshall makes the following distinctions when determining religious freedom:

> First, it refers to the freedoms of particular bodies, houses of worship, humanitarian organisations, educational institutions, and so forth. Second, it refers to freedom for particular individual religious practices – prayer, worship, dress, proclamation, diet, and so forth. Third, it refers to human rights in general in so far as they involve particular religious bodies, individuals, and activities. For example, the freedom to proclaim one's religion or belief is an issue of freedom of speech generally and is parallel to freedom of speech in other areas of life. Similarly, for freedom of the press or freedom of association. This means that we are looking not only at particular 'religious rights' but also at any human right, insofar as it impacts on freedom of religion or belief. In particular, we need to be aware of any different and unequal treatment of particular religions. This means that the question of adverse discrimination needs specific attention.

Marshall also points out however that there are situations where it is not immediately evident that an infringement of a human right is in fact a violation of freedom of religion *per se*:

- A priest acting alone in Central America is killed because of his human-rights work, and he regards such human-rights work as a necessary consequence of his faith. This is not an instance of religious persecution because any other person of a different faith, or no faith, in the same situation would face the same attack. However, if a church has a pastoral policy that includes such human-rights work, then any limits on this are limits on the believing practice of the church and of its clergy, and so are a violation of religious freedom.

- A European country bans Islamic dress in schools. This is a violation of religious freedom since, while the school may legitimately want to enforce a dress code, that should be outweighed by a right to live according to one's religion. If it were a case of a full covering and veil and the school were worried about checking someone's identity, say at exam time, then there might be additional legitimate concerns, but a way could be found around them.

- A country bans polygamy or polyandry whereas some religions allow it. This is not a violation of religious freedom since no religion requires polygamy or polyandry.

- A country has a state church or its equivalent but otherwise allows freedom of religion. This is always an instance of religious discrimination and, therefore, a limit on religious freedom; however, its importance may vary greatly. Does the state fund the church in a way that it does not fund other religious bodies? Does the church have political privileges or privileges in areas such as education?

- A religious group is also a politically separatist group. This can be a very difficult area as states have a legitimate interest in avoiding fragmentation. However, international law also recognizes a 'people's right to self-determination'. The question of whether the repression of such a group is a violation of religious freedom would depend on whether the group had a religious identity and on the justice of their cause.

- Are restrictions on the entrance of missionaries or other religious workers a violation of religious freedom? Not necessarily, as there is no universal right to be able to work in a country other than one's own.

- A decision by a country either to fund or not to fund education by religious groups can be consistent with religious freedom. The question is one of discrimination, that is, whether some groups are denied funds because of their beliefs while others are given funds.

Marshall suggests that, despite the ambiguities of such cases, a number of guidelines present themselves when deciding whether there had been an infringement of specifically religious freedom:

- Are restrictions on religious groups 'reasonable'? In the words of many international human-rights documents, are they 'subject only to such limitations as are prescribed by law and are necessary to protect public safety, order, health, or morals or the fundamental rights and freedom of others'?

- The question of whether something is a violation of religious freedom (as distinct from a violation of some other human right) depends on whether someone's religion is a factor (usually not the only one) in the treatment they give or receive. To put this another way, would someone of different religious beliefs or no religious beliefs in the same situation mete out or suffer the same treatment? (Of course, groups with different beliefs may, by that fact, also not fall into the same situation.)

- Is there discrimination; is different treatment given to different religious groups?

- Religious freedom can be violated by a government or another religious group even if the violation is not itself for religious motives. The *motive is* not, per se, the issue; the key question is, what is the result? If a government represses churches, mosques, and temples in the same way it represses political parties, newspapers, and other groups, simply because the government wants no other centres of loyalty or authority in the society, then this is still a violation of religious freedom.

(Marshall 2000, cited Gearon 2002: 345–356)

References, Further Reading and Research

Ayton-Shenker, Diana (1995) 'The Challenge of Human Rights and Cultural Diversity' (Geneva: United Nations Department of Public Information)
Bloom, Irene, Martin, J. Paul and Proudfoot, Wayne L. (eds) (2000) *Religious Diversity and Human Rights* (New York: Columbia University Press)
Casanova, José (1994) *Public Religions in the Modern World* (Chicago: Chicago University Press)
Forsythe, David P. (2000) *Human Rights in International Relations* (third edition, Cambridge: Cambridge University Press)
Fukuyama, Francis (1992) *The End of History and the Last Man* (London: H. Hamilton)
Gearon, Liam (2002) *Religion and Human Rights: A Reader* (Brighton and Portland: Sussex Academic Press)
Haynes, Jeff (1998) *Religion in Global Politics* (Harlow: Longman)
HRW (2001) *Anti-Racism Summit Ends on Hopeful Note* (New York: Human Rights Watch)

Huntington, Samuel (1992) *The Clash of Civilizations* (Washington, D.C.: American Enterprise Institute)

International Association for Religious Freedom (2001) *Centennial Reflections International Association for Religious Freedom, 1900–2000* (Assen: The Netherlands: Van Gorcum)

Lerner, Nathan, *Religion, Beliefs, and Human Rights* (Maryknoll, New York: Orbis, 2000)

Paul Marshall (ed) (2000) *Religious Freedom in the World: A Global Report on Freedom and Persecution* (London: Broadman and Holman)

Stahnke, Tad, Martin, J. Paul (eds) (1998) *Religion and Human Rights: Basic Documents* (New York: Columbia University Press/Center for the Study of Human Rights)

The Declaration of the Parliament of the World's Religions in Kung, Hans and Schmidt, Helmut *A Global Ethic and Global Responsibilities: Two Declarations* (London: SCM, 1998)

UN (2002) *Elimination of All Forms of Intolerance and Discrimination based on Religion or Belief*, Human Rights Study Series, No 2 (New York: UN)

UN (2002) *Study on the Rights of Persons belonging to Ethnic, Religious or Linguistic Minorities*, Human Rights Study Series, No 5 (New York: UN)

II

Defining and Defending Human Rights

III
Human Solidarity

CHAPTER NINE

Women's Rights

Poverty eradication without empowerment is unsustainable. Everyone is entitled to all the rights and freedoms set forth in this Declaration, without distinction of any kind, such as race, colour, sex, language, religion, political or other opinion, national or social origin, property, birth or other status.
Article 2, Universal Declaration of Human Rights

Our starting point is the recognition that there can be no human rights without women's rights. Mary Robinson, UN High Commissioner for Human Rights

---

Figure 9.1

Background Notes: Defining Women's Rights

Background Notes: Defining Women's Rights

The fourth but most prominent and influential World Conference on Women was held in Beijing in 1995 in the year of the fiftieth anniversary of the founding of the United Nations. The resulting Beijing Declaration was conscious to set the event in the context of other conferences. Cited conferences included those on women in Nairobi in 1985, on children in New York in 1990, on environment and development in Rio de Janeiro in 1992, on human rights in Vienna in 1993, on population and development in Cairo in 1994.

The Beijing Declaration that arose sets the context, tone and agenda for women's rights:

> We, the Governments participating in the Fourth World Conference on Women,
>
> Gathered here in Beijing in September 1995,
>
> Determined to advance the goals of equality, development and peace for all women everywhere in the interest of all humanity,
>
> Acknowledging the voices of all women everywhere and taking note of the diversity of women and their roles and circumstances, honouring the women who paved the way and inspired by the hope present in the world's youth,
>
> Recognize that the status of women has advanced in some important respects in the past decade but that progress has been uneven, inequalities between women and men have persisted and major obstacles remain, with serious consequences for the well-being of all people,
>
> Also recognize that this situation is exacerbated by the increasing poverty that is affecting the lives of the majority of the world's people, in particular women and children, with origins in both the national and international domains,
>
> Dedicate ourselves unreservedly to addressing these constraints and obstacles and thus enhancing further the advancement and empowerment of women all over the world, and agree that this requires urgent action in the spirit of determination, hope, co-operation and solidarity, now and to carry us forward into the next century.

Convinced that 'Women's empowerment and their full participation on the basis of equality in all spheres of society, including participation in the decision-making process and access to power, are fundamental for the achievement of equality, development and peace', the commitments made by the Beijing Declaration included:

- Full implementation of the human rights of women and of the girl child 'as an inalienable, integral and indivisible part of all human rights and fundamental freedoms'
- The empowerment and advancement of women 'including the right to freedom of thought, conscience, religion and belief'.

Broken down, these included a determination to:

- Take effective action against violations of women's basic rights and freedoms
- Eliminate all forms of discrimination against women and the girl child
- Remove all obstacles to gender equality and the empowerment of women
- Encourage participation of men in the development of gender equality
- Promote women's economic independence
- Eradicate the persistent and increasing burden of poverty on women
- Promote people-centred sustainable development, especially by the provision of basic and lifelong education for girls and women
- Ensure peace for the advancement of women
- Prevent and eliminate all forms of violence against women and girls
- Ensure equal access to and equal treatment of women in education
- Ensure equal access to and equal treatment of women health care
- Overcome barriers to women's empowerment through factors such as race, age, language, ethnicity, culture, religion, or disability or indigenous identity
- Respect for international law, including humanitarian law, in order to protect women and girls in particular.

These determinations were declared as part of a will to develop 'the fullest potential of girls and women of all ages, ensure their full and equal participation in building a better world for all and enhance their role in the development process'. For this reason the Beijing Declaration and the Platform for Action which arose stressed the interdependence 'and mutually reinforcing components' of sustainable development, linking women's economic development and social development with environmental protection.

International Legal Standards: Defending Women's Rights

Beijing+5 Process and Beyond was a focus for a meeting in the United States. The twenty-third special session of the General Assembly on 'Women 2000: Gender Equality, Development and Peace for the Twenty-first Century' took place at the United Nations Headquarters in New York from 5 June to 9 June 2000 and adopted a Political Declaration and outcome document entitled 'Further Actions and Initiatives to Implement the Beijing Declaration and Platform for Action'.

Figure 9.2

International Legal Standards: Defending Women's Rights

Convention on the Political Rights of Women (20 December 1952, into effect 7 July 1957)

Declaration on the Protection of Women and Children in Emergency and Armed Conflict (14 December 1974)

Declaration on the Elimination of All Forms of Discrimination against Women (7 November 1967, into effect 3 September 1981)

Convention on the Elimination of All Forms of Discrimination against Women (20 November 1989)

Declaration on the Elimination of Violence against Women (20 December 1993)

Optional Protocol to the Convention on the Elimination of Discrimination against Women (10 December 1999, into effect 22 December 2000)

For full texts of the documents, follow links at **www.unhchr.ch/**

Featured Document: Convention on the Elimination of All Forms of Discrimination against Women (1979)

On 18 December 1979, the *Convention on the Elimination of All Forms of Discrimination against Women* was adopted by the UN General Assembly. It entered into force as an international treaty on 3 September 1981. By the tenth anniversary of the Convention in 1989, close to one hundred nations have signed and agreed to its terms. But this remains under half of the representative nation-states with representative status at the UN. While marking significant progress, and the culmination of three decades of work by UN Commission on the Status of Women (established 1946), the necessity for the Beijing and Beijing+5 meetings shows that the world is far from agreement and the equal status of women remains in many countries a distant ideal, despite the fact that fundamental equality in human rights was foundational to the UN Charter and the Universal Declaration.

The Convention, summarised in Figure 9.3, outlines that discrimination against women is real and extensive and details the areas (health, education, employment, and legal and political status, for instance) where progress needs to be made. The Convention also devotes much time to reproductive rights, issues around maternity and rights centred around marriage. A key area of importance that underpins such rights is the sporadic disparity between the UN definitions of women's rights and those as perceived within cultural and perhaps especially (but not exclusively) religious traditions.

Figure 9.3

Featured Document

Convention on the Elimination of All Forms of Discrimination against Women
Adopted 18 December 1979, entry into force 3 September 1981

PART I: Definitions and Discrimination

Article 1 defines 'discrimination against women' as meaning 'any distinction, exclusion or restriction made on the basis of sex which has the effect or purpose of impairing or nullifying the recognition, enjoyment or exercise by women, irrespective of their marital status, on a basis of equality of men and women, of human rights and fundamental freedoms in the political, economic, social, cultural, civil or any other field'.

Article 2 commits States to condemning 'discrimination against women in all its forms, agree to pursue by all appropriate means and without delay a policy of eliminating discrimination against women and, to this end, undertake':

'(a) To embody the principle of the equality of men and women in their national constitutions or other appropriate legislation if not yet incorporated therein and to ensure, through law and other appropriate means, the practical realisation of this principle
(b) To adopt appropriate legislative and other measures, including sanctions where appropriate, prohibiting all discrimination against women
(c) To establish legal protection of the rights of women on an equal basis with men and to ensure through competent national tribunals and other public institutions the effective protection of women against any act of discrimination
(d) To refrain from engaging in any act or practice of discrimination against women and to ensure that public authorities and institutions shall act in conformity with this obligation
(e) To take all appropriate measures to eliminate discrimination against women by any person, organisation or enterprise
(f) To take all appropriate measures, including legislation, to modify or abolish existing laws, regulations, customs and practices which constitute discrimination against women
(g) To repeal all national penal provisions which constitute discrimination against women.'

Article 3 commits States to 'take in all fields, in particular in the political, social, economic and cultural fields, all appropriate measures, including legislation, to ensure the full development and advancement of women, for the purpose of guaranteeing them the exercise and enjoyment of human rights and fundamental freedoms on a basis of equality with men'.

Article 4 states that special measures aimed at 'accelerating *de facto* equality between men and women shall not be considered discrimination as defined in the present Convention, but shall in no way entail as a consequence the maintenance of unequal or separate standards; these measures shall be discontinued when the objectives of equality of opportunity and treatment have been achieved'. It also states that special measures 'aimed at protecting maternity shall not be considered discriminatory'.

Article 5 commits States to take appropriate measures:

'(a) To modify the social and cultural patterns of conduct of men and women, with a view to achieving the elimination of prejudices and customary and all other practices which are based on the idea of the inferiority or the superiority of either of the sexes or on stereotyped roles for men and women

(b) To ensure that family education includes a proper understanding of maternity as a social function and the recognition of the common responsibility of men and women in the upbringing and development of their children, it being understood that the interest of the children is the primordial consideration in all cases.'

Article 6 commits States to 'take all appropriate measures, including legislation, to suppress all forms of traffic in women and exploitation of prostitution of women'.

PART II: Political Rights

Article 7 commits States to 'take all appropriate measures to eliminate discrimination against women in the political and public life of the country', particularly the right to vote, to be eligible for election, to hold public office and participate in government'.

Article 8 commits States to 'take all appropriate measures to ensure to women, on equal terms with men and without any discrimination, the opportunity to represent their Governments at the international level and to participate in the work of international organisations'.

Article 9 commits States to 'grant women equal rights with men to acquire, change or retain their nationality. They shall ensure in particular that neither marriage to an alien nor change of nationality by the husband during marriage shall automatically change the nationality of the wife, render her stateless or force upon her the nationality of the husband.' It also commits States to 'grant women equal rights with men with respect to the nationality of their children'.

PART III: Education, Health and Employment

Article 10 commits States to ensuring equal rights in education, including career and vocational guidance. This article includes detailed reference to a wide range of measures such as access to the same curricula and examinations. There is a commitment to 'the elimination of any stereotyped concept of the roles of men and women at all levels'. Coeducation is to be encouraged, as too is 'the revision of textbooks and school programmes and the adaptation of teaching methods'.

Article 11 commits States 'to eliminate discrimination against women in the field of employment'. This detailed Article contains reference to work as an 'inalienable right', equality of opportunity of employment at all stages from application onwards and particular rights and protections of women in regard to maternity.

Article 12 commits States to 'take all appropriate measures to eliminate discrimination against women in the field of health care in order to ensure, on a basis of equality of men and women, access to health care services, including those related to family planning'.

Article 13 commits States to 'take all appropriate measures to eliminate discrimination against women in other areas of economic and social life in order to ensure, on a basis of equality of men and women, the same rights, in particular:

(a) The right to family benefits
(b) The right to bank loans, mortgages and other forms of financial credit
(c) The right to participate in recreational activities, sports and all aspects of cultural life.'

Article 14 commits States to 'take into account the particular problems faced by rural women and the significant roles which rural women play in the economic survival of their families'.

PART IV: Legal Rights

Article 15 commits States to 'accord to women equality with men before the law'.

Article 16 commits States to 'take all appropriate measures to eliminate discrimination against women in all matters relating to marriage and family relations', including consent to marry and the 'same rights and responsibilities during marriage and at its dissolution'.

PART V: The Committee on the Elimination of Discrimination against Women

Article 17 establishes the Committee on the Elimination of Discrimination against Women. This is to consist of 'twenty-three experts of high moral standing and competence in the field covered by the Convention'. The elected individual 'shall serve in their personal capacity, consideration being given to equitable geographical distribution and to the representation of the different forms of civilisation as well as the principal legal systems'.

Articles 18 to **22** contains further reference to the terms and conditions of the Committee.

PART VI: Technical Obligations

Article 23 states that 'Nothing in the present Convention shall affect any provisions that are more conducive to the achievement of equality between men and women which may be contained in the legislation of a State Party.'

Article 24 commits States to the 'full realisation of the rights recognized in the present Convention'.

Article 25 concern the signing and ratification of the Convention, **Article 26** its revision, **Article 27** its entering into force, **Article 28** reservations, **Article 29** disputes, **Article 30** its translation.

For a full text of the document, follow links at **www.unhchr.org**

Organisations Concerned with Women's Rights: UN, Committee on the Elimination of Discrimination against Women and NGO

1. UN/ Committee on the Elimination of Discrimination against Women: Committee on the Elimination of Discrimination against Women (CEDAW)

The Committee on the Elimination of Discrimination against Women (CEDAW) was formed through the 1979 Convention. Its formation, duties and basic operational features are defined in Part V, Articles 17–22 of the Convention.

The membership of the Committee (Article 17) consists of 'twenty-three experts of high moral standing and competence in the field covered by the Convention', with considerable detail on electoral procedures presented in numerous subsections of the Article. Article 18 concerns the reporting procedures to the Secretary-General of the United Nations, a year after the Convention coming into force and thereafter every four years. Article 19 allows the Committee freedom to 'adopt its own rules of procedure' but deems that elections of members should take place every two years, with meetings of the Committee (Article 20) to meet annually for at least two weeks. Article 21 determines that the Committee reports annually through the Economic and Social Council to the General Assembly of the UN. The UN Secretary-General is obliged to transmit the reports of the Committee to the Commission on the Status of Women for its information. Article 22 allows the Committee to extend its expertise by inviting specialised agencies to support its work, as these fall within the provisions of the Convention. Figure 9.4 outlines the extent of such additional agencies.

Figure 9.4

Women's Rights: UN Links

United Nations Development Fund for Women (UNIFEM) – New York, USA
www.unifem.undp.org/

Integrating Gender into the Third World Conference against Racism, Racial Discrimination, Xenophobia and Related Intolerance.
www.unifem.undp.org/hr_racism.html

WomenWatch – New York, USA
www.un.org/womenwatch

Division for the Advancement of Women
www.un.org/womenwatch/daw

Documents and Databases
www.un.org/womenwatch/resources

The UN Working for Women
www.un.org/womenwatch/un

UN Conferences and Events
www.un.org/womenwatch/confer

---

2. *Human Rights Watch*

Human Rights Watch is one of the world's leading human rights organisations. A campaigning organisation, one of its distinguishing features is its near-comprehensive annual global – continent-to-continent and country-to-country – reports. Links on the HRW website are easy to follow to any country in the world. Its periodic campaigns also focus on particularly pressing aspects of human rights. In recent years, one of its most important has been 'Against the Trafficking Of Women and Girls'. The following extract sets the context but also highlights how such trafficking not only infringes basic notions of female equality but also how this extreme and inhuman indignity can be seen as a modern form of slavery (see chapter 5):

> Trafficking in persons – the illegal and highly profitable recruitment, transport, or sale of human beings for the purpose of exploiting their labor – is a slavery-like practice that must be eliminated. The trafficking of women and children into bonded sweatshop labor, forced marriage, forced prostitution, domestic servitude, and other kinds of work is a global phenomenon. Traffickers use coercive tactics including deception, fraud, intimidation, isolation, threat and use of physical force, and/or debt bondage to control their victims. Women are typically recruited with promises of good jobs in other countries or provinces, and, lacking better options at home, agree to migrate. Through agents and brokers who arrange the travel and job placements, women are escorted to their destinations and delivered to the employers. Upon reaching their destinations, some women learn that they have been deceived about the nature of the work they will do; most have been lied to about the financial arrangements and conditions of their employment; and all find themselves in coercive and abusive situations from which escape is both difficult and dangerous. (HRW, 2002)

Figure 9.5 lists a number of key HRW documents in this area.

Figure 9.5

Trafficking in Women and Girls: Human Rights Watch Documents

Letter to Secretary Powell regarding the U.S. State Department's Trafficking Report
June 18, 2002

U.S. State Department Trafficking Report Missing Key Data, Credits Uneven Efforts
HRW Press Release, June 6, 2002

A Human Rights Approach to the Rehabilitation and Reintegration into Society of Trafficked Victims
Oral Statement at Conference, May 15–16

Greece: Recommendations Regarding the Draft Law
Briefing Paper, March 8, 2002

Greece: Urgent Action Required on Trafficking
HRW Press Release, July 24, 2001

Trafficking of Migrant Women for Forced Prostitution into Greece
Memorandum of Concern, July 24, 2001

U.S. State Department Trafficking Report Contains Serious Flaws
HRW Press Release, July 12, 2001

Victims of Trafficking and Violence Protection Act of 2000: Trafficking in Persons Report
U.S. State Department Report, July 12, 2001
Text of H.R. 3244, 'Victims of Trafficking and Violence Protection Act of 2000'
300k PDF file, January 24, 2000

Owed Justice: Thai Women Trafficked into Debt Bondage in Japan
Human Rights Watch September 2000 report

HRW Testimony before the U.S. Senate Committee on Foreign Relations Subcommittee on
Near Eastern and South Asian Affairs
February 22, 2000

Full details at **www.hrw.org**

Figure 9.6 presents a selection of other, related HRW reports on women's rights.

Figure 9.6

Women's Rights: Other HRW Reports

*Statement in Support of U.S. Senate Ratification of the Convention on the Elimination of All Forms of
Discrimination Against Women (CEDAW)*
To the Senate Foreign Relations Committee (June 13, 2002)

Reconstruction and Human Rights in Afghanistan
Congressional Human Rights Caucus Members' Briefing (February 14, 2002)

*Recommendations regarding the Proposal for a Council Framework Decision on Combating Traffick-
ing in Human Beings* (Feb. 2001)

Stopping Violence Against Women: A Challenge to Governments (June 2000)

Law of Protection from Family Violence (March 31, 2000)
www.hrw.org

References, Further Reading and Research

Agosin, Marjorie (ed) (2001) *Women, Gender and Human Rights: A Global Perspective* (New Brunswick: NJ: Rutgers
    University Press)
Askin, Kelly D. and Dorean M. Koenig (eds) *Women and International Human Rights Law* (Ardsley, NY: Trans-
    national)
Beigbeder, Yves (2001) *New Challenges for UNICEF: Children, Women and Human Rights* (Basingstoke: Palgrave)
Howland, Courtney (1999) *Religious Fundamentalisms and the Human Rights of Women* (Basingstoke: Macmillan)
HRW (2002) *International Trafficking of Women and Children* (New York: Human Rights Watch)
Human Rights Centre (2000) *Key Points on Women's Human Rights: An Initiative of the Study Group on Women's
    Human Rights* (Colchester: Human Rights Centre, University of Essex)
Jeffries, Alison (ed) (1999) *Women's Voices, Women's Rights*, Oxford Amnesty Lectures (Oxford: Westview)
Kumar, Krishna (ed) (2001) *Women and Civil War: Impact, Organisations and Action* (Boulder and London: Lynne
    Rienner Publishers)

McColgan, Aileen (2000) *Women under the Law: The False Promise of Human Rights* (Harlow: Longman)

Rendel, Margherita (1997) *Whose Human Rights?* (Stoke on Trent: Trentham Books)

Schechter, Michael G. (ed) *United Nations-Sponsored World Conferences: Focus on Impact and Follow-Up* (Tokyo: United Nations University Press)

UN (2000) *The World's Women, 2000: Trends and Statistics* (New York: United Nations)

UN (2002) *Discrimination against Women: The Convention and the Committee* (New York: United Nations)

UN (2002) *Harmful Traditional Practices Affecting the Health of Women and Children*, Fact Sheet 23 (New York: United Nations)

UNICEF (1999) *Human Rights for Children and Women: How UNICEF Makes Them a Reality* (New York: UNICEF)

Wichterich, Christa (2000) *The Globalised Woman: Reports from the Future of Inequality*, trans. Patrick Camiller (London: Zed Books)

CHAPTER TEN

Children's Rights

All wars, disastrous or victorious, are waged against children.
Eglantyne Jebb, Founder of Save the Children

Figure 10.1

Children's Rights: Chapter Headings

Background Notes: Defining Children's Rights

The Summit for Children – with the World Declaration and Plan of Action – held 8–10 May 2002, was a meeting of the UN General Assembly dedicated to the children and adolescents of the world. Providing an opportunity to review progress in the lives of children in the decade since the 1990 World Conference on Children, it brought together government leaders and Heads of State, NGOs, representatives of major UN bodies as well children themselves at the United Nations in New York.

One of the statements arising from the Conference was the *World Declaration on the Survival, Protection and Development of Children* (see **www.unicef.org/wsc/declare**). The adopted plan of action related to this Declaration committed participants to carefully timed targets for achieving improvements in the lives of children around the globe. Meetings like this indicate the high priority given to children rights today. Key target areas included:

- Improving living conditions for children and their chances for survival by increasing access to health services for women and children
- Reducing the spread of preventable diseases
- Creating more opportunities for education
- Providing better sanitation and greater food supply
- Protecting children in danger

According to the UN, the Special Session's global agenda can be summarised by a plan of action to achieve three essential outcomes:

- The best possible start in life for all children.
- A good-quality basic education for all children.
- The opportunities for all children, especially adolescents, to have meaningful participation in their communities.

The Global Movement for Children that resulted from the Conference is designed to be a platform for action that 'will work to provide a united voice for all those throughout the world working to improve the lives of children'. Nelson Mandela and Graça Machel (who wrote an important report in 1996 on children and armed conflict) were among those calling for a partnerships between governments, civil society and the private sector to form a global movement 'committed to ending discrimination against children and adolescents'. The aim of this partnership has the high ideals of changing the world for children in order to 'ensure that every child, without exception, is assured the right to dignity, security and self-fulfilment'. (For more on the Global Movement for Children, see **www.unicef.org/specialsession/about/global-movement**)

All issues of human rights affect children most severely, particularly economic-related rights, such as the right to food, and the rights to health and to education. One of the more disturbing aspects of children's rights has been the use of children in situations of civil unrest and war. As a result of a recommendation of the United Nations Committee on the Rights of the Child, the General Assembly in 1993 requested the Secretary-General to appoint an authority to study the impact of armed conflict on children. Graca Machel, the Secretary-General's appointed expert on the subject and a former Minister for Education in Mozambique, submitted a report, *The Impact of Armed Conflict on Children* to the 1996 session of the General Assembly. The Report suggests that armed conflict 'more than any other force, has transformed the lives of millions of children and women' and that far from simply being caught in the crossfire, many women and children are actually being specifically targeted. Here, the Report chillingly suggests, 'Nothing is spared, held sacred or protected'. According to Human Rights Watch:

> Physically vulnerable and easily intimidated, children typically make obedient soldiers. Many are abducted or recruited by force, and often compelled to follow orders under threat of death. Others join armed groups out of desperation. As society breaks down during conflict, leaving children no access to school, driving them from their homes, or separating them from family members, many children perceive armed groups as their best chance for survival. Others seek escape from poverty or join military forces to avenge family members who have been killed.

> Child soldiers are being used in more than thirty countries around the world. Human Rights Watch has interviewed child soldiers from countries including Angola, Colombia, Lebanon, Liberia, Sierra Leone, Sudan and Uganda. In Sierra Leone, thousands of children abducted by rebel forces witnessed and participated in horrible atrocities against civilians, including beheadings, amputations, rape, and

burning people alive. Children forced to take part in atrocities were often given drugs to overcome their fear or reluctance to fight. (HRW, 2001)

Further, 'because of their immaturity and lack of experience child soldiers suffer higher casualties than their adult counterparts' and 'even after the conflict is over, they may be left physically disabled or psychologically traumatized': 'Frequently denied an education or the opportunity to learn civilian job skills, many find it difficult to re-join peaceful society. Schooled only in war, former child soldiers are often drawn into crime or become easy prey for future recruitment.' (HRW, 2001)

There are some signs of hope. The annual tragedy of child deaths by antipersonnel mines have at least declined since the adoption of the 1997 Mine Ban Treaty. The adoption of the statute for the International Criminal Court holds out some hope of ending the impunity of those who recruit children in armed conflicts and target schools for attack. Yet even if there have been positive developments, for countless children around the world, promises from agreements have been broken:

> The armed conflicts that rage in all quarters of the world have produced appalling abuses of children's rights. Hundreds of thousands of children have been pressed into service as soldiers. Millions have become refugees – displaced from their homes, often separated from their families; their future and safety uncertain. Children living outside war zones may also be subjected to routine violence. Street children on every continent endure harassment and physical abuse by police.

> Millions of children have no access to education, work long hours under hazardous conditions, or languish in orphanages or detention centres where they endure inhumane conditions and daily assaults on their dignity, in violation of the rights guaranteed to them under the Convention. (HRW, 2001)

International Legal Standards: Defending Children's Rights

The range of conventions and declarations outlined in Figure 10.2 reiterate the notion that children's rights are human rights but that their vulnerability makes it necessary for many more general or seemingly unrelated international legal standards to make particular reference to the specific rights of the child or the context of childhood.

Figure 10.2

International Legal Standards: Defending Children's Rights

Declaration on the Rights of the Child (20 November 1959)

Declaration on Social and Legal Principles relating to the Protection and Welfare of Children, with Special Reference to Foster Placement and Adoption Nationally and Internationally (3 December 1986)

Convention on the Rights of the Child (20 November 1989, into effect 2 September 1990)

United Nations Rules for the Protection of Juveniles Deprived of the Liberty (14 December 1990)

United Nations Guidelines for the Prevention of Juvenile Delinquency (The Riyadh Guidelines) (14 December 1990)

Optional protocol to the Convention on the Rights of the Child on the involvement of children in armed conflict (25 May 2000, into effect 12 February 2002)

Optional protocol to the Convention on the Rights of the Child on the sale of children, child prostitution and child pornography (25 May 2000, into effect 18 January 2002)

For full texts of these documents, follow links at **www.un.hchr.org**

Also useful are links to Children in Armed Conflict and Displacement: The Convention, Treaties and International Agreements (CRIN Webpage).

Featured Document: The Convention on the Rights of the Child (1989)

Nevertheless, despite this evident attention given to children across the full range of international human rights standards, the 1989 Convention on the Rights of the Child indicates too the perceived need to give singular attention to young people. The 1989 Convention on the Rights of the Child remains the most single ratified of all such UN conventions. Its principle articles are summarised in Figure 10.3.

Figure 10.3

Convention on the Rights of the Child
20 November 1989, entry into force 2 September 1990

PART I: Children's Rights

Article 1 defines a child as 'every human being below the age of eighteen years unless under the law applicable to the child, majority is attained earlier'.

Article 2 presents States' responsibilities to 'respect and ensure the rights set forth in the present Convention to each child within their jurisdiction without discrimination of any kind, irrespective of the child's or his or her parent's or legal guardian's race, colour, sex, language, religion, political or other opinion, national, ethnic or social origin, property, disability, birth or other status'.

Article 3 states that 'In all actions concerning children, whether undertaken by public or private social welfare institutions, courts of law, administrative authorities or legislative bodies, the best interests of the child shall be a primary consideration.'

Article 4 presents States responsibilities to 'undertake all appropriate legislative, administrative, and other measures for the implementation of the rights recognized in the present Convention. With regard to economic, social and cultural rights, States Parties shall undertake such measures to the maximum extent of their available resources and, where needed, within the framework of international co-operation.'

Article 5 presents the responsibilities of States to 'respect the responsibilities, rights and duties of parents or, where applicable, the members of the extended family or community as provided for by local custom, legal guardians or other persons legally responsible for the child, to provide, in a manner consistent with the evolving capacities of the child'.

Article 6 states that 'Every child has the inherent right to life.' It presents the responsibilities of States to ensure 'the maximum extent possible the survival and development of the child'.

Article 7 outlines the need for the child's birth to be registered immediately: 'the right from birth to a name, the right to acquire a nationality and. as far as possible, the right to know and be cared for by his or her parents'. States have responsibilities to ensure the implementation of these rights 'in accordance with their national law and their obligations under the relevant international instruments' but in particular 'where the child would otherwise be stateless'.

Article 8 presents the responsibilities of States to 'undertake to respect the right of the child to preserve his or her identity, including nationality, name and family relations as recognized by law without unlawful interference'.

Article 9 presents the responsibilities of States to 'ensure that a child shall not be separated from his or her parents against their will, except when competent authorities subject to judicial review determine, in accordance with applicable law and procedures, that such separation is necessary for the best interests of the child. Such determination may be necessary in a particular case such as one involving abuse or neglect of the child by the parents, or one where the parents are living separately and a decision must be made as to the child's place of residence.'

Article 10 deals with 'applications by a child or his or her parents to enter or leave a State', especially 'for the purpose of family reunification' and the need for States to deal with such applications 'in a positive, humane and expeditious manner'.

Article 11 outlines the responsibilities of States to take all measure 'to combat the illicit transfer and non-return of children abroad'.

Article 12 outlines the responsibilities of States to 'assure to the child who is capable of forming his or her own views the right to express those views freely in all matters affecting the child, the views of the child being given due weight in accordance with the age and maturity of the child'.

Article 13 states that 'The child shall have the right to freedom of expression; this right shall include freedom to seek, receive and impart information and ideas of all kinds, regardless of frontiers, either orally, in writing or in print, in the form of art, or through any other media of the child's choice.'

Article 14 states the rights of the child 'to freedom of thought, conscience and religion'.

Article 15 states the rights of the child 'to freedom of association and to freedom of peaceful assembly'.

Article 16 states that 'No child shall be subjected to arbitrary or unlawful interference with his or her privacy, family, home or correspondence, nor to unlawful attacks on his or her honour and reputation.'

Article 17 presents the responsibilities of States to 'recognize the important function performed by the mass media and shall ensure that the child has access to information and material from a diversity of national and international sources, especially those aimed at the promotion of his or her social, spiritual and moral well-being and physical and mental health'.

Article 18 presents the responsibilities of States to 'use their best efforts to ensure recognition of the principle that both parents have common responsibilities for the upbringing and development of the child. Parents or, as the case may be, legal guardians, have the primary responsibility for the upbringing and development of the child. The best interests of the child will be their basic concern.'

Article 19 presents the responsibilities of States to 'take all appropriate legislative, administrative, social and educational measures to protect the child from all forms of physical or mental violence, injury or abuse, neglect or negligent treatment, maltreatment or exploitation, including sexual abuse, while in the care of parent(s), legal guardian(s) or any other person who has the care of the child'.

Article 20 states that 'A child temporarily or permanently deprived of his or her family environment, or in whose own best interests cannot be allowed to remain in that environment, shall be entitled to special protection and assistance provided by the State.'

Article 21 presents the responsibilities of States to 'recognize and/or permit the system of adoption shall ensure that the best interests of the child shall be the paramount consideration'.

Article 22 presents the responsibilities of States to 'take appropriate measures to ensure that a child who is seeking refugee status or who is considered a refugee in accordance with applicable international or domestic law and procedures shall, whether unaccompanied or accompanied by his or her parents or by any other person, receive appropriate protection and humanitarian assistance'.

Article 23 presents the responsibilities of States to 'recognize that a mentally or physically disabled child should enjoy a full and decent life, in conditions which ensure dignity, promote self-reliance and facilitate the child's active participation in the community'.

Article 24 presents the responsibilities of States to 'recognize the right of the child to the enjoyment of the highest attainable standard of health and to facilities for the treatment of illness and rehabilitation of health'. None should be deprived of access to such services. States Parties shall strive to ensure that no child is deprived of his or her right of access to such health care services. The Article also deals with a child's basic rights to have access to related primary health care, the States' responsibilities to combat disease and malnutrition and 'the provision of adequate nutritious foods and clean drinking-water, taking into consideration the dangers and risks of environmental pollution'. The Article outlines in more detail issues related to child health.

Article 25 presents the responsibilities of States to 'recognize the right of a child who has been placed by the competent authorities for the purposes of care, protection or treatment of his or her physical or mental health, to a periodic review of the treatment provided to the child and all other circumstances relevant to his or her placement'.

Article 26 presents the responsibilities of States to 'recognize for every child the right to benefit from social security, including social insurance, and shall take the necessary measures to achieve the full realisation of this right in accordance with their national law'.

Article 27 presents the responsibilities of States to 'recognize the right of every child to a standard of living adequate for the child's physical, mental, spiritual, moral and social development'. The Article also recognizes that 'the parent(s) or others responsible for the child have the primary responsibility to secure, within their abilities and financial capacities, the conditions of living necessary for the child's development'.

Article 28 presents the responsibilities of States to 'recognize the right of the child to education, and with a view to achieving this right progressively and on the basis of equal opportunity'. In particular, this involves making 'primary education compulsory and available free to all', the encouragement of secondary education and making higher education 'accessible to all on the basis of capacity by every appropriate means'.

Article 29 outlines some general comments on the implementation of Article 28.

Here States have responsibilities to ensure General comment on its implementation, including:

'The development of the child's personality, talents and mental and physical abilities to their fullest potential;

The development of respect for human rights and fundamental freedoms, and for the principles enshrined in the Charter of the United Nations;

The development of respect for the child's parents, his or her own cultural identity, language and values, for the national values of the country in which the child is living, the country from which he or she may originate, and for civilisations different from his or her own.'

Article 30 states, 'In those States in which ethnic, religious or linguistic minorities or persons of indigenous origin exist, a child belonging to such a minority or who is indigenous shall not be denied the right, in community with other members of his or her group, to enjoy his or her own culture, to profess and practise his or her own religion, or to use his or her own language.'

Article 31 presents the responsibilities of States to 'recognize the right of the child to rest and leisure, to engage in play and recreational activities appropriate to the age of the child and to participate freely in cultural life and the arts'. It also suggests that States 'shall respect and promote the right of the child to participate fully in cultural and artistic life and shall encourage the provision of appropriate and equal opportunities for cultural, artistic, recreational and leisure activity.'

Article 32 presents the responsibilities of States to 'recognize the right of the child to be protected from economic exploitation and from performing any work that is likely to be hazardous or to interfere with the child's education, or to be harmful to the child's health or physical, mental, spiritual, moral or social development'.

Article 33 presents the responsibilities of States to 'take all appropriate measures, including legislative, administrative, social and educational measures, to protect children from the illicit use of narcotic drugs and psychotropic substances as defined in the relevant international treaties, and to prevent the use of children in the illicit production and trafficking of such substances'.

Article 34 presents the responsibilities of States to 'undertake to protect the child from all forms of sexual exploitation and sexual abuse'.

Article 35 presents the responsibilities of States to 'take all appropriate national, bilateral and multilateral measures to prevent the abduction of, the sale of or traffic in children for any purpose or in any form'.

Article 36 presents the responsibilities of States to 'protect the child against all other forms of exploitation prejudicial to any aspects of the child's welfare'.

Article 37 states that 'No child shall be subjected to torture or other cruel, inhuman or degrading treatment or punishment. Neither capital punishment nor life imprisonment without possibility of release shall be imposed for offences committed by persons below eighteen years of age.'

Article 38 presents the responsibilities of States to 'undertake to respect and to ensure respect for rules of international humanitarian law applicable to them in armed conflicts which are relevant to the child', taking 'all feasible measures to ensure that persons who have not attained the age of fifteen years do not take a direct part in hostilities'.

Article 39 presents the responsibilities of States to 'take all appropriate measures to promote physical and psychological recovery and social reintegration of a child victim of: any form of neglect, exploitation, or abuse; torture or any other form of cruel, inhuman or degrading treatment or punishment; or armed conflicts. Such recovery and reintegration shall take place in an environment which fosters the health, self-respect and dignity of the child.'

Article 40 presents the responsibilities of States to 'recognize the right of every child alleged as, accused of, or recognized as having infringed the penal law to be treated in a manner consistent with the promotion of the child's sense of dignity and worth'.

Article 41 states that 'Nothing in the present Convention shall affect any provisions which are more conducive to the realisation of the rights of the child and which may be contained in the law of a State party or international law in force for that State.'

PART II: Implementation Procedures Monitoring

Article 42 concerns the responsibilities of States 'to make the principles and provisions of the Convention widely known, by appropriate and active means, to adults and children alike'.

Article 43 outlines how for the purpose of 'examining the progress made by States Parties in achieving the realisation of the obligations undertaken in the present Convention, there shall be established a Committee on the Rights of the Child, which shall carry out the functions hereinafter provided'. The remaining 11 of the 12 sub-sections concern the administration of the Committee.

Article 44 presents the responsibilities of States 'to report to the UN about progress on implementation of the Convention'.

Article 45 concerns the effectiveness of the Convention through international collaboration, especially through specialized agencies like the United Nations Children's Fund (UNICEF) 'and other competent bodies' and procedures for the Committee to recommend to the General Assembly to request the Secretary-General to undertake on its behalf studies on specific issues relating to the rights of the child'.

PART III: Other Procedural Matters

Articles 46–54 refer to procedural matters about signing, ratifying, translating and amending the Convention.

For a full text of this document, follow links at **www.unhchr.org**

While, as the World Conference in Vienna recognised, there have been many failures in the implementation in many human rights, the years following the adoption of the Convention on the Rights of the Child have been marked by some significant advances on behalf of children:

> Many countries have used the convention as the basis to revise domestic legislation and improve protections for children, or have appointed special ombudspersons or envoys for children. As the Committee on the Rights of the Child, the body that monitors compliance of states parties to the convention, has evaluated country reports under the convention, it has developed new standards of protection and pressed governments for specific reforms. (HRW, 2001)

The World Summit for Children demonstrates at least goodwill in the global community to achieve a better world for children.

Unfortunately, reality often falls far short of ideals. Of the goals set by such global conferences and UN conventions, one area of failure is in education. Education is a critical factor in eliminating poverty and deprivation. The Global Campaign for Education is an alliance of a number of NGOs – Action Aid, Oxfam and a number of agencies from the developing world – who have challenged the failure to fulfil promise of 'education for all' central to the UN's mandate since the Universal declaration. The Global Campaign for Education particularly challenges the declaration made at the World Education Summit in Dakar in 1990, that no country seriously committed to education for all would be prevented from implementing this through lack of resources. In a paper entitled 'Broken Promises', the Campaign for Global Education summarise the crisis:

> Education is a basic right. It is also the keystone of poverty eradication efforts. Yet more than half a century after this right was enshrined in the UN Declaration, education is in crisis in the world's poorest countries. 125 million children – nearly 60 percent of them girls – are out of primary school.

Many times that number of children receives an education that is so curtailed, or such low quality, that they acquire few of the tools needed to escape poverty. Nearly one billion adults are unable to read and write.

The following is a summary statement of the key areas of concern raised by the Global Campaign for Education:

At the Millennium Summit in 2000, the governments of the world promised concrete steps to tackle this education crisis – since reaffirmed at the Special Session on Children (May 2002) and the World Summit on Sustainable Development (August 2002):

- Gender equality in primary and secondary schools by 2005
- Universal completion of primary education, and a 50% reduction in adult illiteracy, by 2015

Yet without concerted action by both donors and developing countries governments, these promises will be broken. On current trends, the goal of universal primary education will be missed in 88 countries, and 75 million children will remain out of school in 2015. Already, the 2005 goal of gender equity in education appears beyond reach.
(Global Campaign for Education, 2002: 3)

Organisations Concerned with Children's Rights: UN/Regional-Governmental and NGO

1. UN/Regional-Governmental: UNICEF

The United Nations International Children's Emergency Fund (UNICEF) was created by the United Nations General Assembly in 1946 to help children after World War II in Europe. (Yet again, we see the importance of the founding mission of the United Nations within a post-World War two setting.) It was in 1953 that UNICEF became a formal part of the United Nations system, with its humanitarian focus on children extended from Europe to the developing world. Its name was shortened to the United Nations Children's Fund, but the acronym UNICEF was somehow retained.

The United Nations Children's Fund (UNICEF) based in New York (visit: **www.unicef.org**) defines its mission as 'Changing the world with children', emphasising both that children are citizens and therefore partners in the struggle for the fulfilment of their basic human rights. In its self-defined mission, it states: 'UNICEF helps children get the care and stimulation they need in the early years of life and encourages families to educate girls as well as boys. It strives to reduce childhood death and illness and to protect children in the midst of war and natural disaster. UNICEF supports young people, wherever they are, in making informed decisions about their own lives, and strives to build a world in which all children live in dignity and security. Working with national governments, NGOs, other UN agencies and private-sector partners, UNICEF protects children and their rights by providing services and supplies and by helping shape policy agendas and budgets in the best interests of children.' Figure 10.4 indicates how this mission has developed since 1946.

Figure 10.4

The UNICEF website provides an outline history

1946
Food to Europe
After World War II, children in Europe face famine and disease. UNICEF created by the UN to provide emergency aid.

1950
For all the world's children
As Europe recovers after the war, some countries believe UNICEF's job is over, but the United Nations General Assembly extends UNICEF's task to include working with children and families throughout the developing world.

1953
UNICEF becomes permanent part of the United Nations
The beginning of UNICEF's international campaign against yaws, a disfiguring disease affecting millions of children that could be cured with penicillin.

1959
Rights of the child
The UN General Assembly adopts the *Declaration of the Rights of the Child*, focusing on children's rights to education, health care and good nutrition.

1962
Education
In the newly independent African countries, UNICEF supports teacher training and supplies classroom equipment. By 1965, education absorbs 43 percent of UNICEF's assistance to Africa.

1965
Nobel Peace Prize
UNICEF is awarded the 1965 Nobel Peace Prize in Oslo, Norway 'for the promotion of brotherhood among nations'.

1979
International Year of the Child
During this year, marked by celebrations around the world, people and organisations reaffirm their commitment to children's rights.

1981
Breastfeeding Code Approved
The World Health Assembly adopts the International Code of Marketing of Breast Milk Substitutes to stop a decline in breastfeeding.

1983

Child Survival and Development Revolution

UNICEF launches drive to save the lives of millions of children each year through programs that control dehydration, immunize children and support breastfeeding and good nutrition.

1989

Convention on the Rights of the Child

The Convention is adopted by the UN General Assembly. It enters into force in September 1990. It becomes the most widely accepted human rights treaty in history.

1990

World Summit for Children

An unprecedented summit of Heads of State and Government at the United Nations in New York City sets 10-year goals for children's health, nutrition and education.

1996

Children and conflict

A Report of the Expert of the Secretary-General, Ms. Graça Machel: The Impact of Armed Conflict on Children, a study supported by UNICEF.

1998

United Nations Security Council debates children and conflict

The Council's first open debate on the subject reflects the magnitude of international concern for the impact of wars on children.

2001

Say Yes for Children campaign launched

The Global Movement for Children begins mobilizing every citizen of every nation to change the world with children. The Say Yes for Children Campaign builds on this momentum, with millions of children and adults around the world pledging their support for critical actions to improve children's lives.

Further details at **www.unicef.org**

Figure 10.5 provides a sample of useful links to children's rights in global and regional context.

Figure 10.5

Children's Rights: Global/Regional Links

Children's Rights
www.unicef.org/crc/index.html
The State of the World's Children 2000
www.unicef.org/sowc00/uwar2.htm

World Education Forum: Dakar 2000
www.unicef.org/efa/results.htm

The Progress of Nations 2000 – LOST CHILDREN
www.unicef.org/pon00/re.htm
Defence for Children InternationalGuide for NGOs reporting to the Committee on the Rights of the Child
www.defence-for-children.org/

United Nations Educational, Scientific and Cultural Organisation (UNESCO) – Paris, France
www.unesco.org/

---

2. NGO: Save the Children

Save the Children was formed in informal circumstances in New York City during the time of an urgent crisis affecting the mountain poor of the Appalachians during Depression hit America in the winter of 1932. But it identifies its roots in the international children's rights movement started in England in 1919 at the end of the First World War, and with Eglantyne Jebb, the founder of the British Save the Children Fund. Today, Save the Children works in over forty-five countries worldwide. One of its major focuses is on children in emergency and crisis situations:

- Children affect by war and displacement
- Children affected by HIV/AIDS
- Exploited Children (trafficking, working children and street children)

One of its major recent campaigns has been on involving corporate sponsors to get involved in their work, shrewdly selling the positive benefits to corporate image for doing so. And much of its work continues – for example the 'Every Mother, Every Child' initiative – to highlight the inextricable link between children and their mothers. Given the historical American lineage, one of its more unsuspected areas of appeal is to tackle the poverty of large numbers of children in the United States. The details of 'America's Forgotten Children' are outlined in Figure 10.6.

Figure 10.6

America's Forgotten Children

Life is extremely hard for children growing up in poverty in the United States, regardless of where they live. Opportunities to grow and thrive are limited by inadequate education, poor health care and a lack of quality jobs for parents. The resulting damage often leaves a deep scar on children, decreasing their chances of succeeding in school, getting good jobs, and living a healthy life.

Would you be surprised to learn that child-poverty rates are actually *higher* in rural America than in urban America? They are – in fact, about 2.5 million children live in poverty in rural areas of the United States. For children in remote rural areas, poverty can be particularly devastating. Health care, childcare, education and other key services don't even exist in some communities, requiring hours of travel. As a result, many families can't meet their children's most basic needs.

To focus attention on these issues, Save the Children has released its report to the nation, America's Forgotten Children: Child Poverty in Rural America. The study reveals the critical issues facing poor children who live in remote and forgotten parts of America and the extraordinary obstacles they have to overcome. The report also serves as a call to action for government, corporations and foundations to work together to refocus the nation's efforts on alleviating poverty's draining impact on rural children. We must build:

- Human capital – provide incentives to train the people who are in the community, and attract people with the skills needed to help serve children
- Community institutions – create and strengthen comprehensive community centers and other places that serve children and youth
- Economic self-sufficiency for families – ensure that welfare-to-work policies make the needs of children a priority
- Support systems for pockets of poverty – target and increase public and private support to reach children in the poorest rural areas.

Save the Children is using America's Forgotten Children: Child Poverty in Rural America to launch a national campaign for rural children that will reach policymakers at the federal, state, and county levels. Save the Children addresses these issues through our Web of Support. programs. Web of Support is a proven and successful community partnership approach that provides children with caring adults, safe places and constructive activities during their out-of-school time in the areas of health, education and economic opportunity.

Further details at **www.savethechildren.org**

References, Further Reading and Research

Beigbeder, Yves (2001) *New Challenges for UNICEF: Children, Women and Human Rights* (Basingstoke: Palgrave)
Department for International Development (2000) *Working in Partnership with the United Nations Children's Fund* (UNICEF)
Drew, Sandhya (2000) *Children and the Human Rights Act* (London: Save the Children)
HRW (2001) *Children's Rights and War* (New York: Human Rights Watch)
Landsdown, Gerison (2001) *Children's Rights: A Second Chance* (London: Save the Children)
Landsdown, Gerison (2001) *Promoting Children's Participation in Democratic Decision Making* (Florence: UNICEF)
Man, Nathalie (2000) *Children, Torture and Power: The Torture of children by States and Armed Opposition Groups* (London: Save the Children)
Seabrook, Jeremy (2001) *Children of Other Worlds: Exploitation in the Global Market* (London: Pluto Press)
UN (2002) *The Rights of the Child*, Fact Sheet 10 (New York: United Nations)
UN (2002) *Harmful Traditional Practices Affecting the Health of Women and Children* (New York: United Nations)
UN (2002) *The Family in International and Regional Human Rights Instruments* (New York: United Nations)
UN (2002) *Sexual Exploitation of Children*, Human Rights Studies Series No. 8 (New York: United Nations)
UNICEF (2000) *The UN Convention on the Rights of the Child* (London: UK Committee for UNICEF)

CHAPTER ELEVEN

The Rights of Indigenous Peoples

Historians and academics agree that the colonisation of the New World saw extreme expressions of racism – massacres, forced-march relocations, the 'Indian wars', death by starvation and disease. Today, such practices would be called ethnic cleansing and genocide.

Erica Irene Daes, United Nations Working Group on Indigenous Peoples *'Doctrines of Dispossession' – Racism against Indigenous Peoples*

Exploration and colonisation beginning in the fifteenth century not only led to rapid appropriation of indigenous peoples' lands and natural resources, but also despoiled their sciences, ideas, arts and cultures. For indigenous peoples all over the world the protection of their cultural and intellectual property has taken on growing importance and urgency. They cannot exercise their fundamental human rights as distinct nations, societies and peoples without the ability to control the knowledge they have inherited from their ancestors.

UN Fact Sheet No. 9, The Rights of Indigenous Peoples

Figure 11.1

The Rights of Indigenous Peoples: Chapter Headings

Background Notes: Defining the Rights of Indigenous Peoples

Who are indigenous peoples? Though sparsely distributed, indigenous, tribal or aboriginal peoples inhabit vast areas of the earth's surface, numbering according to the United Nations approximately 300 million. They are so-called 'because they were living on their lands before settlers came from elsewhere; they are the descendants of those who inhabited a country or a geographical region at the time when people of different cultures or ethnic origins arrived, the new arrivals later becoming dominant through conquest, occupation, settlement or other means'.

Since time immemorial, different tribal groups have competed for land and resources. Over the past five or six centuries as Europeans began a process of colonisation that lasted for half a millennium, pressure on indigenous peoples intensified as never before. Small but ancient groups have been historically very vulnerable in the history of colonisation. When in the mid to late twentieth century formal colonialism began to decline the new postcolonial states continued to exert a negative influence on indigenous peoples, almost without exception. And today, according to the United Nations, 'Indigenous peoples belong to the poorest and most vulnerable on earth':

> Although they differ among themselves in terms of economic development and the extent to which they have been able to preserve their cultural autonomy and economic independence, many indigenous societies share common characteristics. Most societies and communities have maintained their own distinct cultural traditions, and continue to speak their own languages, which are, for the most part, unwritten. As a result they have rarely completely assimilated within the national societies in which they live. Instead, they often live in subordinate positions within national societies. They generally inhabit marginal and inhospitable territories. Many of them survive through hunting and gathering and/or practising pastoralism or subsistence farming.
>
> Despite these common characteristics, there does not exist any single accepted definition of indigenous peoples that captures their diversity. Therefore, self-identification as indigenous or tribal group is a fundamental criterion for determining whether groups are indigenous or tribal, sometimes in combination with other variables such as 'language spoken' and 'geographic location or concentration'. (UN, 2002)

Indigenous peoples are represented on most of the planet's continents, and many risk disappearance.

International Legal Standards: Defending the Rights of Indigenous Peoples

Early attempts by indigenous peoples to gain protection of their rights in a world still dominated by colonising powers were extremely unsuccessful. With the Universal declaration of Human Rights in 1948, the rights of indigenous people have generally been subsumed under related rights; for example, those dealing with minorities, slavery and forced labour. A turning-point came in 1970, when the Sub-Commission on Prevention of Discrimination and Protection of Minorities recommended that a comprehensive study be made of the problem of discrimination against indigenous populations. Other international statements followed – see Figures 11.2 and 11.3.

Figure 11. 2

International Legal Standards: Defending the Rights of Indigenous Peoples

Right of self-determination

Declaration on the Granting of Independence to Colonial Countries and Peoples (14 December 1960)

General Assembly resolution 1803 (XVII) of 14 December 1962, 'Permanent sovereignty over natural resources' (14 December 1962)

Prevention of discrimination
Equal Remuneration Convention (29 June 1951, into effect 23 May 1953)
Discrimination (Employment and Occupation) Convention (15 June 1960)
Convention against Discrimination in Education (14 December 1960)
Protocol Instituting a Conciliation and Good Offices Commission to be responsible for seeking a settlement of any disputes which may arise between States Parties to the Convention against Discrimination in Education (10 June 1962, into effect 24 October 1968)
United Nations Declaration on the Elimination of All Forms of Racial Discrimination (20 December 1962)
International Convention on the Elimination of All Forms of Racial Discrimination (21 December 1965)
International Convention on the Suppression and Punishment of the Crime of *Apartheid* (30 November 1973)
Declaration on Race and Racial Prejudice (27 November 1978)
Declaration on the Elimination of All Forms of Intolerance and of Discrimination based on Religion or Belief (25 November 1981)
Declaration on the Rights of Persons Belonging to National or Ethnic, Religious and Linguistic Minorities (18 December 1992)

Employment
ILO Convention (No. 169) concerning Indigenous and Tribal Peoples in Independent Countries (21 June 1989, into effect 5 September 1991)

For full texts of these documents, follow links at **www.un.unhchr.org**

Featured Document: United Nations Draft Declaration on the Rights of Indigenous Peoples (1994)

The most significant piece of relevant international human rights documentation is the UN Draft Declaration on the Rights of Indigenous Peoples, as yet in draft.

Figure 11.3

UN Draft Declaration on Indigenous and Tribal Rights (1994)

PART I

Article 1 states that, 'Indigenous peoples have the right to the full and effective enjoyment of all human rights and fundamental freedoms recognized in the Charter of the United Nations, the Universal Declaration of Human Rights and international human rights law.'

Article 2 states that 'Indigenous individuals and peoples are free and equal to all other individuals and peoples in dignity and rights, and have the right to be free from any kind of adverse discrimination, in particular that based on their indigenous origin or identity.'

Article 3 states that 'Indigenous peoples have the right of self-determination. By virtue of that right they freely determine their political status and freely pursue their economic, social and cultural development.'

Article 4 states that 'Indigenous peoples have the right to maintain and strengthen their distinct political, economic, social and cultural characteristics, as well as their legal systems, while retaining their rights to participate fully, if they so choose, in the political, economic, social and cultural life of the State.'

Article 5 states that 'Every indigenous individual has the right to a nationality.'

PART II

Article 6 states that 'Indigenous peoples have the collective right to live in freedom, peace and security as distinct peoples and to full guarantees against genocide or any other act of violence, including the removal of indigenous children from their families and communities under any pretext.'

Article 7 states that 'Indigenous peoples have the collective and individual right not to be subjected to ethnocide and cultural genocide', this to include prevention of redress for such action directed against them.

Article 8 states that 'Indigenous peoples have the collective and individual right to maintain and develop their distinct identities and characteristics, including the right to identify themselves as indigenous and to be recognized as such.'

Article 9 states that 'Indigenous peoples and individuals have the right to belong to an indigenous community or nation, in accordance with the traditions and customs of the community or nation concerned. No disadvantage of any kind may arise from the exercise of such a right.'

Article 10 states that 'Indigenous peoples shall not be forcibly removed from their lands or territories. No relocation shall take place without the free and informed consent of the indigenous peoples concerned and after agreement on just and fair compensation and, where possible, with the option of return.'

Article 11 states that 'Indigenous peoples have the right to special protection and security in periods of armed conflict.'

PART III

Article 12 states that 'Indigenous peoples have the right to practise and revitalize their cultural traditions and customs.' This includes 'the right to maintain, protect and develop the past, present and future manifestations of their cultures, such as archaeological and historical sites, artefacts, designs, ceremonies, technologies and visual and performing arts and literature'. It also includes 'the right to the restitution of cultural, intellectual, religious and spiritual property taken without their free and informed consent or in violation of their laws, traditions and customs'.

Article 13 states that 'Indigenous peoples have the right to manifest, practise, develop and teach their spiritual and religious traditions, customs and ceremonies; the right to maintain, protect, and have access in privacy to their religious and cultural sites; the right to the use and control of ceremonial objects; and the right to the repatriation of human remains.' This Article also recognises States responsibilities to preserve, respect and protect sacred indigenous sites.

Article 14 states that 'Indigenous peoples have the right to revitalize, use, develop and transmit to future generations their histories, languages, oral traditions, philosophies, writing systems and literatures, and to designate and retain their own names for communities, places and persons.'

PART IV

Article 15 states that 'Indigenous children have the right to all levels and forms of education of the State. All indigenous peoples also have this right and the right to establish and control their educational systems and institutions providing education in their own languages, in a manner appropriate to their cultural methods of teaching and learning.' The Article also gives States responsibilities to ensure that indigenous children living outside their communities are 'provided access to education in their own culture and language'.

Article 16 states that 'Indigenous peoples have the right to have the dignity and diversity of their cultures, traditions, histories and aspirations appropriately reflected in all forms of education and public information.' States have responsibilities 'in consultation with the indigenous peoples . . . to eliminate prejudice and discrimination and to promote tolerance, understanding and good relations among indigenous peoples and all segments of society'.

Article 17 states that 'Indigenous peoples have the right to establish their own media in their own languages. They also have the right to equal access to all forms of non-indigenous media.' States have responsibilities 'to ensure that State-owned media duly reflect indigenous cultural diversity'.

Article 18 states that 'Indigenous peoples have the right to enjoy fully all rights established under international labour law and national labour legislation.'

PART V

Article 19 states that 'Indigenous peoples have the right to participate fully, if they so choose, at all levels of decision-making in matters which may affect their rights, lives and destinies through representatives chosen by themselves in accordance with their own procedures, as well as to maintain and develop their own indigenous decision-making institutions.'

Article 20 states that 'Indigenous peoples have the right to participate fully, if they so choose, through procedures determined by them, in devising legislative or administrative measures that may affect them.'

Article 21 states that 'Indigenous peoples have the right to maintain and develop their political, economic and social systems, to be secure in the enjoyment of their own means of subsistence and development, and to engage freely in all their traditional and other economic activities. Indigenous peoples who have been deprived of their means of subsistence and development are entitled to just and fair compensation.'

Article 22 states that 'Indigenous peoples have the right to special measures for the immediate, effective and continuing improvement of their economic and social conditions, including in the areas of employment, vocational training and retraining, housing, sanitation, health and social security.' This Article addresses the special concerns of 'indigenous elders, women, youth, children and disabled persons'.

Article 23 states that 'Indigenous peoples have the right to determine and develop priorities and strategies for exercising their right to development. In particular, indigenous peoples have the right to determine and develop all health, housing and other economic and social programmes affecting them and, as far as possible, to administer such programmes through their own institutions.'

Article 24 states that 'Indigenous peoples have the right to their traditional medicines and health practices, including the right to the protection of vital medicinal plants, animals and minerals. They also have the right to access, without any discrimination, to all medical institutions, health services and medical care.'

PART VI

Article 25 states that 'Indigenous peoples have the right to maintain and strengthen their distinctive spiritual and material relationship with the lands, territories, waters and coastal seas and other resources which they have traditionally owned or otherwise occupied or used, and to uphold their responsibilities to future generations in this regard.'

Article 26 states that 'Indigenous peoples have the right to own, develop, control and use the lands and territories, including the total environment of the lands, air, waters, coastal seas, sea-ice, flora and fauna and other resources which they have traditionally owned or otherwise occupied or used. This includes the right to the full recognition of their laws, traditions and customs, land-tenure systems and institutions for the development and management of resources, and the right to effective measures by States to prevent any interference with, alienation of or encroachment upon these rights.'

Article 27 states that 'Indigenous peoples have the right to the restitution of the lands, territories and resources which they have traditionally owned or otherwise occupied or used, and which have been confiscated, occupied, used or damaged without their free and informed consent. Where this is not possible, they have the right to just and fair compensation. Unless otherwise freely agreed upon by the peoples concerned, compensation shall take the form of lands, territories and resources equal in quality, size and legal status.'

Article 28 states that 'Indigenous peoples have the right to the conservation, restoration and protection of the total environment and the productive capacity of their lands, territories and resources, as well as to assistance for this purpose from States and through international cooperation. Military activities shall not take place in the lands and territories of indigenous peoples, unless otherwise freely agreed upon by the peoples concerned.' The Article also presents States' responsibilities to 'take effective measures to ensure that no storage or disposal of hazardous materials shall take place in the lands and territories of indigenous peoples' and to take effective measures to ensure, as needed, that programmes for monitoring, maintaining and restoring the health of indigenous peoples, as developed and implemented by the peoples affected by such materials, are duly implemented'.

Article 29 states that 'Indigenous peoples are entitled to the recognition of the full owner-ship, control and protection of their cultural and intellectual property.' They also have 'the right to special measures to control, develop and protect their sciences, technologies and cultural manifestations, including human and other genetic resources, seeds, medicines, knowledge of the properties of fauna and flora, oral traditions, literatures, designs and visual and performing arts'.

Article 30 states that 'Indigenous peoples have the right to determine and develop priori-ties and strategies for the development or use of their lands, territories and other resources.' This includes the responsibility of States to 'obtain their free and informed con-sent prior to the approval of any project affecting their lands, territories and other resources, particularly in connection with the development, utilisation or exploitation of mineral, water or other resources. Pursuant to agreement with the indigenous peoples con-cerned, just and fair compensation shall be provided for any such activities and measures taken to mitigate adverse environmental, economic, social, cultural or spiritual impact.'

PART VII

Article 31 Indigenous peoples, as a specific form of exercising their right to self-determina-tion, have the right to autonomy or self-government in matters relating to their internal and local affairs, including culture, religion, education, information, media, health, housing, employment, social welfare, economic activities, land and resources management, environ-ment and entry by non-members, as well as ways and means for financing these autonomous functions.

Article 32 states that 'Indigenous peoples have the collective right to determine their own citizenship in accordance with their customs and traditions. Indigenous citizenship does not impair the right of indigenous individuals to obtain citizenship of the States in which they live.'

Article 33 states that 'Indigenous peoples have the right to promote, develop and maintain their institutional structures and their distinctive juridical customs, traditions, procedures and practices, in accordance with internationally recognized human rights standards.'

Article 34 states that 'Indigenous peoples have the collective right to determine the responsibilities of individuals to their communities.'

Article 35 states that 'Indigenous peoples, in particular those divided by international borders, have the right to maintain and develop contacts, relations and cooperation, includ-ing activities for spiritual, cultural, political, economic and social purposes, with other peoples across borders.' States have the responsibility to 'take effective measures to ensure the exercise and implementation of this right'.

Article 36 states 'Indigenous peoples have the right to the recognition, observance and enforcement of treaties, agreements and other constructive arrangements concluded with States or their successors, according to their original spirit and intent, and to have States honour and respect such treaties, agreements and other constructive arrangements. Conflicts and disputes which cannot otherwise be settled should be submitted to competent international bodies agreed to by all parties concerned.'

PART VIII

Article 37 give States responsibility to 'take effective and appropriate measures, in consultation with the indigenous peoples concerned, to give full effect' to the provisions of the Declaration.

Article 38 states that 'Indigenous peoples have the right to have access to adequate financial and technical assistance, from States and through international cooperation, to pursue freely their political, economic, social, cultural and spiritual development and for the enjoyment of the rights and freedoms' recognized in the Declaration.

Article 39 states that 'Indigenous peoples have the right to have access to and prompt decision through mutually acceptable and fair procedures for the resolution of conflicts and disputes with States, as well as to effective remedies for all infringements of their individual and collective rights.'

Articles 40 and **41** concern the responsibility that the United Nations has in ensuring the effective implementation of the Declaration.

PART IX

Article 42 states that 'The rights recognized herein constitute the minimum standards for the survival, dignity and well-being of the indigenous peoples of the world.'

Article 43 states that 'All the rights and freedoms recognized herein are equally guaranteed to male and female indigenous individuals.'

Article 44 states that 'Nothing in this Declaration may be construed as diminishing or extinguishing existing or future rights indigenous peoples may have or acquire.'

Article 45 states that 'Nothing in this Declaration may be interpreted as implying for any State, group or person any right to engage in any activity or to perform any act contrary to the Charter of the United Nations.'

For the full text, follow links at **www.unhchr.org**

The United Nations Declaration on the Rights of Indigenous Peoples represents one of the most important developments in the promotion and protection of their basic rights and fundamental freedoms. The Declaration also foresees mutually acceptable and fair procedures for resolving conflicts between indigenous peoples and powerful nation states. It constitutes the minimum standards for the survival and well-being of the world's indigenous peoples.

Organisations Concerned with Indigenous Rights: UN/Regional-Governmental and NGO

1. UN/Regional-Governmental: Working Group on the Rights of Indigenous Peoples

Meetings between the UN and interested NGOs led in 1982 to the formation of the United Nations Working Group on Indigenous Populations (the term 'populations' was changed to 'peoples' in 1988). Answerable ultimately to the Economic and Social Council, this Working Group is a subsidiary organ of the Sub-Commission on Prevention of Discrimination and Protection of Minorities. Its five members – one from each geopolitical region of the world – are independent experts and are members of the Sub-Commission. The Working Group meets for one week immediately before the annual session of the Sub-commission in Geneva.

The need for a new approach and more decisive action to the issue of indigenous peoples was recognized by the General Assembly when, by its resolution of 18 December 1990, it proclaimed 1993 the International Year of the World's Indigenous People. Pressure for such recognition had long come from indigenous peoples themselves. It is a sad fact, indicative of the domination of powerful nations at the UN, that it was not until 1993, at the opening ceremony for the International Year of the World's Indigenous People, that any indigenous leader had directly addressed the General Assembly.

The objective of the Year was to strengthen international cooperation for the solution of problems faced by indigenous peoples in such areas as human rights, the environment, development, education and health. The theme for the year was 'Indigenous peoples – a new partnership'. According to the UN it was aimed at 'the development of a new and equitable relationship between the international community, States and indigenous peoples based on the participation of indigenous people in the planning, implementation and evaluation of projects affecting their living conditions and future'. It was timely that the second World Conference on Human Rights was held in the same year, in Vienna.

Many hundreds of indigenous people attended the conference and their representatives addressed the plenary session. The Vienna Declaration recognized the 'inherent dignity and the unique contribution of indigenous people to the development and plurality of society'. It also reaffirmed 'the commitment of the international community to their economic, social and cultural well-being and their enjoyment of the fruits of sustainable development'. The conference called upon States to 'take concerted positive steps to ensure respect for all human rights and fundamental freedoms of indigenous people, on the basis of equality and non-discrimination, and recognise the value and diversity of their distinct identities, cultures and social organisation'. The conference also recommended that an international decade of the world's indigenous people be proclaimed (1994–2005). An objective of the Decade was 'the promotion and protection of the rights of indigenous people and their empowerment to make choices which enable them to retain their cultural identity while participating in political, economic and social life, with full respect for their cultural values, languages, traditions and forms of social organisation'. Another achievement of the Vienna Conference was a permanent forum for indigenous people in the United Nations system.

Indigenous peoples are entitled to enjoy all existing human rights established since the founding Universal Declaration of Human Rights. The Working Group on Indigenous and Tribal Peoples recognizes, however, that many of the issues of importance to these groups are distinctive. As such, the Working Group on Indigenous and Tribal Groups has a specific mandate to:

• facilitate dialogue between Governments and indigenous peoples
• review national developments pertaining to the promotion and protection of the human rights and fundamental freedoms of indigenous peoples
• develop international standards concerning the rights of indigenous peoples, taking account of both the similarities and the differences in their situations and aspirations throughout the world.

In the 1990s, the Working Group produced a draft declaration which on indigenous and tribal rights to the Sub-Commission on Prevention of Discrimination and Protection of Minorities. On 26 August 1994, the draft was adopted and submitted it to the Commission on Human Rights, as outlined in Figure 11.3, above.

Also critically important have been the three World Conferences to Combat Racism and Racial Discrimination, convened by the United Nations. All of these have focused in one way or another on the particular problems by some of world's most vulnerable minorities – indigenous and tribal peoples. The first two were in Geneva in 1978 and 1983. These debated aspects of discrimination against indigenous peoples and of programmes of action. Some of these principles are reflected in the draft declaration on the rights of indigenous peoples. The most recent conference against racism was in a post-apartheid South Africa in 2001. A list of key dates is summarised in Figure 11.4.

Figure 11.4

The Rights of Indigenous and Tribal Peoples: Key Dates

1948: Universal Declaration of Human Rights
1970: Sub-Commission on Prevention of Discrimination and Protection of Minorities recommends a study of discrimination against indigenous populations
1977: First International Conference of Non-Governmental Organisations on Indigenous Issues, Geneva
1978: First United Nations World Conference to Combat Racism and Racial Discrimination, Geneva
1981: Second International Conference of Non-Governmental Organisations on Indigenous Peoples, Geneva
1982: Formation of the United Nations Working Group on Indigenous Populations.
1983: Second United Nations World Conference to Combat Racism and Racial Discrimination, Geneva
1963: Convention on the Elimination of All Forms of Racial Discrimination
1989: International Labour Organisation Convention Concerning Indigenous and Tribal Peoples
1990: General Assembly proclaims 1993 the International Year of the World's Indigenous People

1993: United Nations World Conference on Human Rights, Vienna

1994: Sub-Commission on Prevention of Discrimination and Protection of Minorities adopts the Draft Declaration on Indigenous and Tribal Rights

1995: Proposed permanent forum for indigenous peoples at the United Nations.

2001: Third United Nations World Conference against Racism, Racial Discrimination, Xenophobia and Related Intolerance, Durban, South Africa

1994–2005: International Decade of the World's Indigenous Peoples

Figure 11.5 provides some key links to the UN and indigenous and tribal peoples.

Figure 11.5

Links: UN and the Rights of Indigenous Peoples

Office of the High Commissioner for Human Rights
www.unhchr.ch
Indigenous Populations and/or Minorities
www.ifad.org/evaluation/public
International Labour Organisation (ILO) – Geneva, Switzerland
www.ilo.org

Research documents:
The Search For Identity, Ethnicity, Religion and Political Violence
www.unrisd.org/engindex/publ/list/op/op6/op06-03
Ethnic Violence Conflict Resolution and Cultural Pluralism
www.unrisd.org/engindex/publ/list/conf/eth1/eth1-04
Ethnic Diversity and Public Policy Overview
www.unrisd.org/engindex/publ/list/op/op8/op08-05
United Nations Educational, Scientific and Cultural Organisation (UNESCO) – Paris, France
www.unesco.org
Multiculturalism
www.unesco.org/most/most1
Linguistic rights
www.unesco.org/most/ln1
Religious rights
www.unesco.org/most/rr1
Cultural heritage
www.unesco.org/culture/heritage
Intercultural dialogue and pluralism
www.unesco.org/culture/dial
United Nations documents and studies on indigenous issues
www.unhchr.ch.huridocda/huridoca.nsf

2. NGO: Survival

Today more than fifteen NGOs concerned with indigenous peoples have consultative status with the United Nations entitling them to contribute to a wide range of international and inter-governmental conferences. These NGOs include:

- Aboriginal and Torres Strait Islander Commission
- Asociacion Kunas Unidos por Nabauana
- Four Directions Council
- Grand Council of the Crees (of Quebec)
- Indian Council of South America
- Indian Law Resource Centre
- Indigenous World Association
- International Indian Treaty Council
- International Organisation of Indigenous Resource Development
- Inuit Circumpolar Conference
- National Aboriginal and Islander Legal Services Secretariat
- National Indian Youth Council
- Saami Council
- Sejekto Cultural Association of Costa Rica
- World Council of Indigenous Peoples

In addition, hundreds of representatives of other indigenous peoples participate in United Nations meetings and contribute to the Working Group on Indigenous Populations. NGOs with general human rights interests – groups like Amnesty International and Human Rights Watch – also actively promote indigenous peoples' rights.

There are an extensive number of NGOs working with indigenous peoples based in the West. Founded in 1969, Survival is probably the world's foremost organisations supporting tribal peoples through public campaigns, education and dissemination of information about tribal groups. It was founded after an article by Norman Lewis in the UK's *Sunday Times* highlighted the massacres, land thefts and genocide taking place in Brazilian Amazonia. Like many modern atrocities, the events in South America took place in the name of 'economic growth'.

Today, Survival has supporters in 82 countries. It works for tribal peoples' rights in three complementary ways: campaigns, education and funding. We work closely with local indigenous organisations and focus on tribal peoples who have the most to lose, usually those most recently in contact with the outside world. Campaigns are not only directed at governments but at 'companies, banks, extremist missionaries, guerrilla armies, museums, narrow-minded conservationists and anyone else who violates tribal peoples' rights'. All their work is rooted in direct personal contact with hundreds of tribal communities. In every respect land is the most crucial problem in relation to the rights of these peoples. Conflict may come from mining by nation states or multi-national companies, development projects (however well-intentioned) and even, as we have seen, environmentalism and tourism. In all these cases, just as the land and its riches were the motivation for colonialism, so land is crucial for the survival of tribal and indigenous peoples today.

If land is central to indigenous and tribal identity, then the most critical threat is of the land's exploitation. The fullest declaration of the potential for exploitation of tribal land – tribal lands are often rich in mineral and other natural wealth – is in the Convention Concerning

Indigenous and Tribal Peoples, approved by the International Labour Organisation (ILO) in a meeting at Geneva in 1989. The ILO has had a long and close association with the United Nations. (Follow links to indigenous rights on **www.ilo.org**)

However, the protection of the rights of indigenous peoples presents particular problems. There is often a conflict between the economic needs of growing populations in the 'mainstream' of nation states, especially the need for basic development, and protection of the environment of tribal peoples. In the developed world, there is great pressure to protect the remaining wilderness of the world. Indigenous peoples do not always see the issue of land use and environmental conservation in the same way. Some of the issues are highlighted through the two case studies in Figures 11.6 and 11.7.

Figure 11.6

Tribal rights versus environmental rights

In the developed world, conservationists tend to be regarded as caring individuals (or organisations) committed to protecting the environment and improving the quality of life on the planet. But the world's tribal peoples sometimes see them rather as a threat.

For many tribal peoples, conservation imposed from outside has meant eviction from their ancestral lands. Many conservationists still believe that to protect nature one must create wilderness areas which are devoid of human habitation. Yet almost all the areas they designate as 'wildernesses' have been inhabited by human beings for thousands of years. This idea of nature as wilderness provides a convenient cover for government programmes of forced assimilation.

In Sri Lanka, for example, the Wanniya-laeto (meaning 'forest-dwellers') or Veddahs, as they are popularly known, are the country's last aboriginal inhabitants. They were evicted from the Madura Oya National Park in 1983. A mainly hunter-gatherer people, most were forced to become rice-cultivating peasants, causing them confusion and misery, with one small group who remained in the forest constantly harassed by officials and the police. Their presence on their ancestral lands became 'illegal', as did their entire way of life because hunting, and the gathering of honey, plants and roots (all crucial to their survival) were against park regulations. Throughout the world, there are similar instances of tribal peoples displaced, or threatened with removal, from their ancestral lands through the creation of 'protected' areas. Many Maasai who formerly lived in what are now the 'game reserves' of East Africa such as Amboseli and Ngorongoro have suffered in this way.

One way of avoiding conflicts between indigenous peoples and conservation is to stop creating protected areas on indigenous territory and instead seek recognition of tribal land rights. In the past ten years many environmentalists have come to the conclusion that the best way of ensuring conservation is to secure indigenous land ownership. In the Amazon region, notably in Brazil, Colombia, Ecuador, Peru and Bolivia, much more land has been recognised as indigenous territories than as protected areas. Unfortunately this has not always stopped logging, mining and oil companies from exploiting and damaging tribal peoples' territories.

Survival believes that some of the forces that are destroying tribal communities (eg. logging, agri-forestry, ranching, mining, oil extraction and dams) are the same ones destroying the environment. Solutions to environmental problems can only emerge by working with local tribal peoples who are directly affected.

For further details, follow links at **www.survival-international.org**

In 1992, the United Nations endorsed a study on measures that should be taken by the international community to strengthen respect for the cultural and intellectual property of indigenous peoples. The study completed by the Economic and Social Council was submitted to the Sub-Commission on Human Rights in August 1993. It is regarded as the 'first formal step in responding to the concerns expressed by indigenous peoples and as a basis for appropriate standard-setting to provide them with some immediate relief from the widespread and growing threats to the integrity of their cultural, spiritual, artistic, religious and scientific traditions'.

In order to protect the heritage of indigenous peoples wider dialogue is need between indigenous peoples and the agencies of the United Nations, bodies such as the United Nations Educational, Scientific and Cultural Organisation (UNESCO), and the World Intellectual Property Organisation (WIPO). The dangers posed to indigenous rights and lifestyles by de-forestation and mining of tribal lands has been well documented. The worlds of indigenous peoples is fragile and vulnerable in other ways, for example by the apparently innocuous pleasures of travel, as outlined by Survival in Figure 11.6.

Figure 11.7

Tourism: The New Imperialism

Tourism was almost certainly the largest global industry by the year 2000.

Mass tourism has been the target of the most criticism. Because it is so large-scale, it places an undue burden on local resources, skews the labour market and increases prices for goods and property in the area. This may create increased hardship for the local population and breed resentment. In response to the more obvious negative effects of tourism, many tour operators have now proclaimed themselves to be 'green' and jumped on the eco-tourism bandwagon. The exact definition of eco-tourism is a matter of considerable debate. It is certainly not clear that eco-tourism provides solutions to the problems caused by tourism.

Tourism Concern is an organisation which monitors the impact of tourism on Third World countries and ensure responsible tourism, has published a charter for sustainable tourism. The aim of the charter is to promote tourism that is just, sustainable and participatory. Eco-tourism should do the following:

* avoid waste and over-consumption
* use local resources sustainably
* maintain and encourage natural, economic, social and cultural diversity
* be sensitive to the host culture
* involve the local community in planning and decision-making

- assess environmental, social and economic impact as a prerequisite to developing tourism
- ensure that most of the benefits go to the local community and avoid over-dependency on tourism as the only industry
- market tourism responsibly, respecting local natural and cultural environments
- train staff in responsible tourism
- monitor impacts of tourism and ensure open disclosure of information.

Tourist interest can sometimes encourage a cultural revival, protecting people's historic and cultural heritage. Many North American Indians earn much needed income through tourism projects which they have set up and run themselves. Siberian peoples, notably in Kamchatka, are doing the same. Indigenous people, with their unique knowledge of the area, play a key role as local guides.

For further details, follow links at **www.survival-international.org**

References, Further Reading and Research

Gayim, Eyassu (1994) *The UN Draft Declaration on Indigenous Peoples: Assessment of the Draft Prepared by the Working Group on Indigenous Populations* (Rovaniemi: University of Lapland)

Gedicks (2001) *Resource Rebels: Native Challenges to Mining and Oil Corporations* (Cambridge, MA: South End Press)

Grim, John A. (ed) (2001) *Indigenous Traditions and Ecology: The Interbeing of Cosmology and Community* (Cambridge, MA: Harvard University Press)

Kirky, Diane and Coleborne (2001) *Law, History and Colonialism: The Reach of Empire* (Manchester: Manchester University Press)

Thornbury, Patrick (2002) *Indigenous Peoples and Human Rights* (Manchester: Manchester University Press)

Meijknecht, Anna (2001) *Towards International Personality: The Position of Minorities and Indigenous Peoples in International Law* (Antwerpen: Intersentia-Hart)

UN (2002), *The Rights of Indigenous Peoples,* Fact Sheet No. 9 (New York: United Nations)

UN (2002) *The Impact of Mercenary Activities on the Right of Peoples to Self-Determination*, Fact Sheet No. 28 (New York: United Nations)

UN (2002) *Study on the Rights of Persons belonging to Ethnic, Religious and Linguistic Minorities*, Human Rights Study Series No. 5 (New York: United Nations)

UN (2002) *Protection of the Heritage of Indigenous Peoples*, Human Rights Study Series No. 10 (New York: United Nations)

Wade, Davis (2001) *Light at the Edge of the World: A Journey through the Realm of Vanishing Cultures* (London: Bloomsbury)

III

Further Challenges for
Human Rights

CHAPTER TWELVE

Human Rights Education

Everyone has the right to education.
Article 26, Universal Declaration of Human Rights

Figure 12.1

Human Rights Education: Chapter Headings

Background Notes: Defining Human Rights Education

The preamble to the United Nations Universal Declaration of Human Rights premises its statement upon the need for effective dissemination of knowledge and understanding of basic human rights, freedoms and linked responsibilities. While education is a basic human right, human rights education is about the provision and development of awareness about fundamental rights, freedoms and responsibilities.

In paragraph 32 of its summary declaration, the World Conference on Human Rights at Vienna (1993) reaffirmed the importance of 'ensuring the universality, objectivity and non-selectivity of the consideration of human rights issues':

> . . . States are duty-bound, as stipulated in the Universal Declaration of Human Rights and the International Covenant on Economic, Social and Cultural Rights and in other international human rights instruments, to ensure that education is aimed at strengthening the respect of human rights and fundamental freedoms. The World Conference on Human Rights emphasizes the importance of incorporating the subject of human rights education programmes and calls upon States to do so. Education should promote understanding, tolerance, peace and friendly relations between the nations and all racial or religious groups and encourage the development of United Nations activities in pursuance of these objectives. *Therefore, education on human rights and the dissemination of proper information,*

both theoretical and practical, play an important role in the promotion and respect of human rights with regard to all individuals without distinction of any kind such as race, sex, language or religion, and this should be integrated in the education policies at the national as well as international levels. (paragraph 33, emphasis added)

Education was and remains central to the 'full and effective implementation of United Nations activities to promote and protect human rights' and 'to this end, United Nations human rights activities should be provided with increased resources (paragraph 35).

The Vienna World Conference also recognised that 'resource constraints and institutional inadequacies may impede the immediate realisation of these objectives' (paragraph 33). It argued that increased efforts should be made 'to assist countries which so request to create the conditions whereby each individual can enjoy universal human rights and fundamental free-doms. Governments, the United Nations system as well as other multilateral organisations are urged to increase considerably the resources allocated to programmes aiming at the establish-ment and strengthening of national legislation, national institutions and related infrastructures which uphold the rule of law and democracy, electoral assistance, human rights awareness through training, teaching and education, popular participation and civil society'. States were called upon to increase attention to such human rights education programmes. In paragraph 36, the necessity of this was affirmed by the recognition of the 'constructive role played by national institutions for the promotion and protection of human rights, in particular in their advisory capacity to the competent authorities, their role in remedying human rights violations, in the dissemination of human rights information, and education in human rights'. It argued that national institutions were best placed to frame programmes for human rights education according to local circumstances.

In England, for example, major developments have taken place in the development of the human rights education through the new National Curriculum subject of citizenship, statutory in secondary schools since August 2002. In citizenship, human rights is now a compulsory element of secondary school education and appears in the requirement for pupils to under-stand 'the legal and human rights and responsibilities underpinning society, basic aspects of the criminal and civil justice system, and how both relate to young people'. Human rights also appears in a number of other areas of citizenship:

• The regional diversity of national, regional religious and ethnic identities in the United Kingdom and the need for mutual respect and understanding
• The work of parliament, the government and the courts in making and shaping the law
• The importance of playing an active part in democratic and electoral processes
• The United Kingdom's relations in Europe, including the European Union, and with the Commonwealth and the United Nations

(For a fuller account of Citizenship in England, follow relevant links at **www.qca.gov.org** and/or **www.dfes.gov.uk**)

In consciousness of the importance of education about human rights, and perhaps a belated recognition of a failure in effective dissemination of general public awareness of human rights, the United Nations declared 1994–2005 as the decade of Human Rights Education. The United Nations thus now maintains an international database on human rights education, pro-viding information on relevant organisations, materials and programmes. The database itself constitutes a contribution to the UN Decade for Human Rights Education (1995–2004). It aims to facilitate information-sharing on the resources available in the area of human rights education. The database is divided into five interdependent sections:

- General (which shows all database documents together)
- Institutions (type, name, address, contact person, etc.)
- Programmes (type, description, target audience, etc.)
- Materials (bibliographic and substantive information)
- Scholarships (funding organisation, admission requirements, etc.)

(Follow the relevant links under **www.unhchr.ch/hredu.nsf**)

Organisations Concerned with Human Rights Education: UN/Regional-Governmental and NGO

1. UN/Regional-Governmental: UN Decade of Human Rights Education

Regional arrangements play a fundamental role in promoting and protecting human rights. They should reinforce universal human rights standards as contained in international human rights instruments, and their protection. The World Conference on Human Rights endorsed 'efforts under way to strengthen these arrangements and to increase their effectiveness, while at the same time stressing the importance of cooperation with the United Nations human rights activities'. The World Conference on Human Rights reiterated too 'the need for regional and sub-regional arrangements for the promotion and protection of human rights where they do not already exist'.

There was a summary of national initiatives undertaken during the Decade for Human Rights Education (1995–2004). Information was received by the Office of the UN High Commissioner for Human Rights (OHCHR) from Governments around the mid-way period of the decade. National initiatives are presented by country, under five regions (Africa; Arab countries; Asia/Pacific; Europe and North America; Latin America and the Caribbean). A very selective international sample is presented here to give something of the flavour of initiatives. It is worthy of note that many of the countries where human rights abuses were widespread, for example, under former dictatorships, now present the most detailed programmes of human rights. Other countries where human rights records remain highly problematic have either not entered upon programmes of human rights education or have not updated past entries.

What the information provides is a useful summary of regional and national developments in human rights education during the decade dedicated to this theme. This includes whether states have been attentive to the Decade's Plan of Action which 'provides for the establishment, upon the initiative of Governments or other relevant institutions, of a national committee for human rights education. This committee should consist of a broad coalition of governmental and non-governmental actors and should be responsible for developing and implementing a comprehensive (in terms of outreach), effective (in terms of educational strategies) and sustainable (over the long term) national plan of action for human rights education, in consultation with regional and international organisations. Such a plan should constitute an integral part of the overall national plan of action for human rights, when applicable, or should be complementary to it.' This call for the establishment of such plans 'has been reiterated both by the General Assembly and the Commission on Human Rights'. More information available at: **www.hredatabase.hchr@unog.ch**. Selected international responses are shown in Figures 12.3–12.7.

Figure 12.3

International Plans for Human Rights Education: AFRICA

Central African Republic

The Ministry of Justice, in close cooperation with MINURCA, organized a national seminar on "The impact of human rights in the national reconstruction process" in May/June 1999. This project was elaborated with the view to adopt a national plan of action for human rights education and promotion. The seminar gathered more than 200 participants,who included Government Officials, and members of political parties, religious communities, NGOs and the civil society.

There is no national plan of action in operation, however OHCHR and the Human Rights Department of the Bureau des Nations Unies en Centrafrique (BONUCA) are working together on a plan [for its adoption]. The introduction of human rights education in schools coupled with the adoption of a national plan are the goals envisaged for the next five years of the Decade at the national level.

Since its creation in November 1999, the Human Rights High Commission has disseminated information and organized seminars directed at all classes of society. A national committee has not been established, however there are plans to do so at the beginning of the academic year 2000/01.

Chad

A national committee for human rights education was established on 8 May 1998, in accordance with decision number 002/PM/98. The Prime Minister acted on a proposal from the National Human Rights Committee (CNDH). The aforementioned decision did not determine the mandate of the committee, however it is anticipated that the following functions will be included:

• the development of education in the human rights domain
• the adoption of an educational system which embraces peace and democracy
• to ensure that human rights concerns are promoted increasingly at all levels of society
• the strengthening of cooperation between OHCHR, African Commission on Human Rights and Populations, the Human Rights Centre, as well as all institutions and inter-governmental organisations in the area of human rights

The committee is comprised of eleven members in total, with six representatives from the following human rights associations:

• Ligue Tchadienne des droits de l'homme (LTDH)
• The Chad Section of the International Observatory
• Chad Non-Violence
• L'association jeunesse anti-clivage
• The Chad Fundamental Rights Association
• The Association for Defense and Promotion of Human Rights

There are also five representatives from the following ministerial departments:
- Justice
- Family and Social Affairs
- National Defense
- Public Affairs
- Higher Education

A plan of action, which is expected to include the following principal actors:
- National Human Rights Committee
- National Education Committee
- Human Rights NGOs
- Government

Figure 12.4

International Plans for Human Rights Education: ARAB COUNTRIES

Egypt

Following a National Conference on the Development of Primary-level Curricula in 1993 and of Preparatory-level Curricula in 1994, the Centre for the Development of Curricula and Teaching Materials began incorporating human rights, and in particular the rights of the child, women's human rights and the prevention of discrimination against women, in these two levels of formal education. The approach chosen was the infusion of these issues in all school subjects and textbooks rather than the creation of separate classes. As a result of meetings organized with human rights specialists, the infusion is taking place through varying courses of action: the incorporation of human rights in all schoolbooks, and the development of accompanying fascicles for students, containing practical activities, and teaching manuals for teachers. In addition, training courses for teachers relating to appropriate teaching strategies have been organized.

Jordan

Jordan has informed OHCHR of a project for the introduction of human rights terms and concepts into school curricula. This has led to the establishment of a committee of human rights experts (including representatives of the Ministry of Education and specialists in human rights), organizing a workshop on human rights to be attended by drafters of curricula, the surveying of existing textbooks to determine how human rights are presented, and the preparation of training materials and aids for school personnel and reference sources for students.

Figure 12.5

International Plans for Human Rights Education: ASIA/PACIFIC

Australia

In December 1998, the Attorney General announced the establishment of a National Committee for Human Rights Education, which brings together the expertise of business, community organisations and the Government in an endeavour to enhance human rights education in Australia.

The Government provided seed funding for the Committee, whose work-plan includes: conducting a comprehensive audit of human rights education needs of the Australian Community; identifying and assessing current initiatives in human rights education; developing a national action plan for human rights education in Australia, focusing on priority needs; providing assistance in the development of comprehensive and effective human rights education programmes in priority areas, in consultation with education delivery agencies; developing effective communication strategies for human rights education; communicating with international agencies and counterparts in other countries to make available best techniques and resources; supporting human rights education initiatives addressing Asia-Pacific needs; developing effective partnerships between Government, business and community sectors; reviewing implementation and reporting progress. No national Plan of Action has been developed as yet.

India

The Government of India has constituted a Coordination Committee, under the chairmanship of the Home Secretary, comprising of secretaries of other ministries and departments. The Committee requested the National Human Rights Commission to draft a national plan of action for human rights education. Priority areas have been identified and include: the introduction of human rights education at undergraduate and postgraduate levels; the inclusion of a qualification in human rights for recruitment in various professional categories; the preparation of training materials and organisation of training courses for professional and other groups, such as members of the security forces, doctors, lawyers, judicial officers, government officials, politicians, non-governmental organisations personnel, trade unionists, members of religious organisations and village level functionaries, and the organisation of debates and seminars on human rights for the general public.

Japan

The Headquarters for the Promotion of Human Rights Education was established in December 1995. In July 1997, a broad national plan of action for human rights education was released, which included the promotion of human rights education and training at all levels (school, general public, corporations and civil society movements, professionals), specific programmes for special groups (women, children, the aged, people with disabilities, people with HIV infection), and the promotion of international cooperation and other public information activities, such as symposia and conferences.

The Headquarters, which is Japan's national committee, is composed of a chairperson (the Prime Minister), a vice-chairperson (the Chief Cabinet Secretary), the Minister of Justice, the Minister for Foreign Affairs, the Minister of Education, Science, Sports and Culture, the Director General of the Management and Coordination Agency Members, the Deputy Chief Cabinet Secretary, and administrative vice-ministers of all the ministries and agencies. The total number of members is 28. There are no NGO representatives on the committee as the objective of establishing committees under the Cabinet is to encourage each of the administrative agencies to exercise their administrative functions and to promote certain measures in a coordinated manner.

Several non-governmental organisations, such as the International Movement Against All Forms of Discrimination and Racism/Japan Committee, the Buraku Liberation League, the National Dowa Educators Association, the Japan Teachers Union and the International Human Rights NGO network, have been actively involved in these initiatives. This includes the elaboration of the Plan, the organisation of training programmes and symposia, and the production of publications.

Figure 12.6

International Plans for Human Rights Education:
EUROPE AND NORTH AMERICA

Canada
Canada has prepared and is making available to the public a thematic and country by country human rights report, based on United Nations sources, entitled *For the Record*.

On the occasion of the 50th Anniversary of the Universal Declaration of Human Rights, the federal Department of Canadian Heritage, in partnership with provincial ministries of education and non-governmental organisations, delivered several human rights awareness campaigns and programmes aimed at all ages. The Canadian Human Rights Commission also advised that human rights education is a regular part of its work and that it would support the establishment of a national plan, if such an initiative were undertaken in Canada.

France
A National Committee for Human Rights Education and Training has been established jointly by the National Commission for UNESCO and the National Consultative Commission for Human Rights. It includes representatives from eleven relevant Ministries, such as Justice, Education, Defence, Foreign Affairs, Social Affairs, Interior, Culture, Youth and Humanitarian Action. Its mandate consists of:

- conducting a survey on past/current activities in the area of human rights education
- assessing needs
- elaborating a plan of action

Four working groups have been constituted within the Committee to assess the state of human rights education in the following areas: primary and secondary schools; universities and higher education; adult education, including several professional groups (police, armed forces, judges, teachers, social workers); and activities undertaken by NGOs, associations and trade unions. The Committee presented a report on the civic and human rights education curricula at the secondary school level, which illustrates the pedagogical objectives, and the contents and reference materials for such courses. It is also organizing a series of colloquia (2001/2003) for experts and educators on various human rights education issues.

Germany

The Government of Germany informed the Office that its contribution to the Decade is focusing on three areas. The first is human rights education in schools. The Basic Law, Lander Constitutions, laws, legal and administrative regulations, and several resolutions of the Conference of Ministers of Education and Cultural Affairs, specify human rights education as one of the educational objectives in all federal states, even where those states have sovereignty over their school systems. Accordingly, human rights education is deeply rooted in a number of subjects in schools, of all types and at all levels. Secondly, a public relations and information campaign, aimed at encouraging the integration of foreigners and the dismantling of mutual prejudices among citizens, has commenced. This is accomplished through an information service, editorial services for local newsletters, radio programmes for foreigners and Germans, and seminars for people working with foreigners. Finally, some development cooperation projects aim at creating learning conditions, which will enable broad sections of the population to gain an insight into social and administrative processes, and thus to exercise their rights.

Turkey

In May 1998, the Human Rights Coordinating High Committee adopted the 'Regulation on the establishment of the National Committee for the Decade for Human Rights Education' and established a national advisory committee for the Decade. The committee consists of representatives of the Prime Minister's Office, the Ministries of Justice, the Interior, Foreign Affairs, National Education, Health, and Culture, four representatives of relevant voluntary institutions, and academics with experience in this field. In July 1999, the National Committee published the Human Rights Education Programme of Turkey (1998–2007) that is composed of the following parts:

* introductory chapters
* priorities of human rights education in Turkey and main target groups
* present state of human rights education and relevant proposals of the National Committee, directed to the following sectors: primary
* schools, high schools and universities
* law enforcement officers attached to the Ministry of Justice
* law enforcement officers attached to the Ministry of Internal Affairs
* the mass media NGOs.

Among the activities mentioned, there are:
* the training of trainers for civil society entities and for the police
* the inclusion of human rights issues in in-service training and entrance examinations for civil service posts

- the conduct of research on human rights concepts, with the support of UNESCO
- various awareness-raising activities
- The programme is now being implemented in cooperation with different partners, including intergovernmental organisations (United Nations, Council of Europe) and civil society organisations.

Figure 12.7

International Plans for Human Rights Education:
LATIN AMERICA AND THE CARIBBEAN

Argentina

Argentina designated the National Direction for the Promotion of Human Rights, within the Office of the Under Secretary of Social and Human Rights, of the Ministry of Interior, a focal point for human rights education. Through a project of technical cooperation established with OHCHR, it has carried out, in collaboration with non-governmental organisations, a series of activities. These include:

- training courses on human rights for teachers aimed at the establishment of a national network of teachers for human rights education
- the dissemination of human rights documents, such as the Vienna Declaration and Programme of Action, the Universal Declaration of Human Rights and the Convention on the Rights of the Child
- the establishment of a publicly accessible National Documentation Centre
- the preparation and dissemination of a bibliography on human rights education, which has been distributed to all educational establishments, governmental and non governmental agencies, libraries and international organisations
- human rights training for police officials and trainers workshops on human rights and the penitentiary system
- human rights training for lawyers and other members of the legal profession
- the establishment of a series of agreements with provincial and national universities in order to carry out joint projects
- the production of a publication on human rights.

Recent activities have included:

- human rights training for administration of justice officials (police, security forces, judges), teachers and governmental officials
- conclusion of cooperation agreements with private and public universities and organisation of joint initiatives
- development of education plans at the provincial level
- special events, such as school competitions, conferences and sports games
- public dissemination of the Universal Declaration, also through a television and radio campaign

Chile

Chile forwarded some general information on human rights education in schools. The establishment of an interministerial committee for the Decade is under consideration. The Ministry of Education in Chile has informed the Office that some related activities have been undertaken at the school level, such as the implementation of the education and democracy and women programmes, which include the dissemination of human rights pedagogical materials in schools, the training of teachers and the organisation of school competitions.

The Educational Reform currently being undertaken in order to include, within the school system, education for democracy, peace and
human rights, involves four specific areas:

- programmes for improvement and pedagogical innovation
- curricular reform
- professional development of teachers
- Full-Time School Day

In addition, relevant complementary extracurricular activities are envisaged.

Human rights are a component of curricula at all educational levels. At university, specific courses on human rights are offered to students in various areas. There is also an initiative, which aims at educating children from indigenous groups both in their language and in Spanish. Specific activities were undertaken, as follows:

- national competition of students on human rights education (1992)
- international seminar on methodologies for human rights education (1993)
- specialized course on human rights education for education supervisors (1993–1994)
- national seminar on human rights education (1994–1995)
- design of methodological tools for human rights education (1993–2000)
- national essay competition 'Jorge Millas Annual Prize' for intellectuals and writers (1993–2000)

El Salvador

In April 1999, a National Committee for Human Rights Education was established, with the objective to formulate and implement a National Plan of Action for Human Rights Education. The committee was also created to improve relations between the Government, inter-government organisations, NGOs, professionals, individuals and civil society in general. The following are a list of the committee's functions:

- to develop and approve a National Plan of Action having held national consultations
- to develop and approve regular action plans
- to authorize activities, including those that are not expressly included in the Plan of Action
- to conduct the activities included in the Plan of Action
- to initiate the participation of different sectors of El Salvadorian society
- to delegate activities to institutions or organisations that are active in the committee, or request the cooperation of other entities or persons
- to receive and authorize the report of activities
- to allocate resources so that activities may be conducted

- to modify the present guidelines and instructions
- to deal with anything that may be considered relevant to the area

Objectives of the Plan of Action are:

- to consolidate the national reconciliation
- to promote the culture of peace based on the respect of human rights and fundamental freedoms
- to prevent human rights violations, survey vulnerable sectors and to prevent potential agents from committing human rights violations
- to promote democracy, sustainable development, the importance of law and the protection of the environment and peace

The main topics:

- basic conceptual aspects of human rights
- fundamental rights
- democratic rights
- the rights of victims of crimes and abuse of power
- rights of women
- rights of children
- rights of elderly people
- right to a healthy environment
- duties of man

The targets:

- the formal education system
- staff of the department of justice
- the public administration
- civil society
- NGOs
- Labour organisations
- Community organisations

Principal Activities:

- undertake consultations regarding the human rights education plan of action
- undertake analysis of human rights education in El Salvador
- promote, stimulate and support development of education in the area of human rights
- sensitize the state departments and civil society to human rights
- organize a campaign to disseminate information regarding human rights and the culture of peace
- set up libraries and documentation centres dealing specifically with human rights
- promote a culture of peace
- award persons and institutions for their work in the area of human rights and culture of peace

Source, and for further exemplars of national models for human rights education across the world, follow links to **www.unhchr.org** and **www.hredatabase.hchr@unog.ch**.

---

2. NGO: Human Rights Watch Academic Freedom Committee

Human Rights and Education has a dual aspect. First, there is the stated right to education. Second, there are rights to fundamental freedom that can be infringed within an academic context (whether school or university). UNESCO's primary but not exclusive educational focus is on the first rather than the second. (By way of exception, in 2000 UNESCO funded a project called NEAR, the network of Education and Academic Rights which looked at and was designed as an alert system to protect academic freedoms within schools and universities worldwide. Its launch was at UNESCO's Paris headquarters.) Human Rights Watch is one amongst a number of organisations that increasingly recognise that academic institutions have been relatively neglected as a potential target for human rights abuses. This aptly illustrates the notion of the indivisibility and interdependence of human rights. For example, the targeting by militia of school-age children is an infringement not just of rights set forth in the Convention on Children's Rights (1989) but also of the more generic right to education. The silencing (extra-judicial killing, false imprisonment) of an academic who offends a State government is potentially an infringement of an entire range of social and cultural rights (freedom of expression, freedom of religion and belief) as well as fundamental civil and political rights.

Formerly known as the Committee for International Academic Freedom (established 1991), the Human Rights Watch Academic Committee brings together staff from the New York-based NGO and 'academic leaders and prominent scholars'. The aim of the Committee and associated programme is 'to monitor, expose, and mobilize concerted action to challenge threats to academic freedom worldwide, and to foster greater scholarly and media attention to the critical role played by institutions of higher education in the promotion of human rights and the development and preservation of civil society':

> Educators, researchers and students are frequent targets of state-sponsored violence and repression. In the most notorious cases, governments bent on imposing a monolithic state ideology have disproportionately targeted teachers and educated individuals for imprisonment, torture and murder. More commonly, governments use intimidation, physical abuse and imprisonment to silence campus-based critics and dissidents, and censor teaching, research and publication on important subjects. Many governments also continue to deny equal access to educational institutions to women and members of disfavoured minority groups.

> Academic freedom work at Human Rights Watch is based on the recognition that such violations have received too little attention in the international human rights community. The academic freedom program seeks to address this deficiency through casework on behalf of embattled academics, collaborative efforts with other human rights organisations and concerned professional associations, thematic research and reports, and publication of an annual overview of violations in the Human Rights Watch World Report.

For more information on the work of the Human Rights Watch Academic Committee, visit the Human Rights Watch website and follow the relevant links. The reporting of the work is divided into the following categories:

- Casework
- Academic Freedom Committee

- Collaborative Efforts
- Thematic Research and Report
- World Reports (since 2000)

Visit **www.hrw.org/advocacy/academic**

References, Further Reading and Research

Davies, Lynn (2000) *The EURIDEM Project: A Review of Pupil Democracy in Europe* (London: Children's Rights Alliance for England)

UN (2000) *Lessons for Life*, Series on the United Nations Decade for Human Rights Education, (1995–2004), No. 1 (New York: United Nations)

UN (2000) *Human Rights Education and Human Rights Treaties*, Series on the United Nations Decade for Human Rights Education (1995–2004), No. 2 (New York: United Nations)

UN (2000) *The Right to Human Rights Education*, Series on the United Nations Decade for Human Rights Education (1995–2004), No. 3 (New York: United Nations)

UN (2000) *ABC – Teaching Human Rights: Practical Activities for Primary and Secondary Schools*, Series on the United Nations Decade for Human Rights Education (1995–2004), No. 4 (New York: United Nations)

UN (2002) *Pocket Guide on Basic Human Rights Instruments* (New York: United Nations)

UN (2002) *Human Rights – A Basic Handbook for UN Staff* (New York: United Nations)

UN (2002) *Human Rights and Social Work: A Manual for Schools of Social Work and the Social Work Profession*, Professional Training Series No. 1 (New York: United Nations)

UN (2002) *Human Rights and Elections: A Handbook on the Legal, Technical and Human Rights Aspects of Elections*, Professional Training Series No. 2 (New York: United Nations)

UN (2002) *Human Rights and Pre-Trail Detention: a Handbook of International Standards relating to Pre-Trial Detentions*, Professional Training Series No. 3 (New York: United Nations)

UN (2002) *National Human Rights Institutions: A Handbook on the Strengthening of National Institutions for the Promotion and Protection of Human Rights*, Professional Training Series No. 4 (New York: United Nations)

UN (2002) H*uman Rights and Law Enforcement: A Manual on Human Rights Training for the Police*, Professional Training Series No. 5 (New York: United Nations)

UN (2002) *International Human Rights Standards for Law Enforcement: A pocket Book on Human Rights for the Police*, Professional Training Series No. 5.1 (New York: United Nations)

UN (2002) *Human Rights Training: A Manual on Human Rights Training Methodology*, Professional Training Series No. 6 (New York: United Nations)

UN (2002) *Training Manual on Human Rights Monitoring*, Professional Training Series No. 7 (New York: United Nations)

UN (2002) *The Istanbul Protocol: Manual on the Effective Investigation and Documentation of Torture and Other Cruel, Inhuman or Degrading Treatment or Punishment*, Professional Training Series No. 8 (New York: United Nations)

Appendix 1

Material available at the Office of High Commissioner for Human Rights
Visit **www.unhchr.ch/html/menu6**

OHCHR
General Materials and Activities

Guidelines for National Plans of Action for Human Rights Education

Summary of national initiatives undertaken within the framework of the Decade for Human Rights Education (1995–2004)

Training and Education Material

Full list of OHCHR Publications

Database on Human Rights Education and Training

– Universal Declaration of Human Rights in more than 300 languages
– Worldwide Collection of Universal Declaration of Human Rights Materials
– More than 50 ideas for commemorating the Universal Declaration of Human Rights
Assisting Communities Together (ACT) Project – Funding human rights education and training activities of civil society

Advisory Services and Technical Cooperation in the Field of Human Rights

Documents: Declarations, Conventions and Treaties

Charter of the United Nations (1945)

International Bill of Human Rights (Fact Sheet 2, Rev.1)
Universal Declaration of Human Rights (10 December 1948)
International Covenant on Economic, Social and Cultural Rights (16 December 1966, into effect 3 January 1976)
International Covenant on Civil and Political Rights (16 December 1966, into effect 23 March 1976)
Optional Protocol to the International Covenant on Civil and Political Rights (16 December 1966, into effect 23 March 1976)
Second Optional Protocol to the International Covenant on Civil and Political Rights, aiming at the abolition of the death penalty (15 December 1989)

Human Rights Defenders
Declaration on the Right and Responsibility of Individuals, Groups and Organs of Society to

Promote and Protect Universally Recognized Human Rights and Fundamental Freedoms (8 March 1999)

Proclamation of Teheran
Proclamation of Teheran (13 May 1968)

Right of self-determination
Declaration on the Granting of Independence to Colonial Countries and Peoples (14 December 1960)
General Assembly resolution 1803 (XVII) of 14 December 1962, 'Permanent sovereignty over natural resources' (14 December 1962)

Prevention of discrimination
Equal Remuneration Convention (29 June 1951, into effect 23 May 1953)
Discrimination (Employment and Occupation) Convention (15 June 1960)
Convention against Discrimination in Education (14 December 1960)
Protocol Instituting a Conciliation and Good Offices Commission to be responsible for seeking a settlement of any disputes which may arise between States Parties to the Convention against Discrimination in Education (10 June 1962, into effect 24 October 1968)
United Nations Declaration on the Elimination of All Forms of Racial Discrimination (20 December 1962)
International Convention on the Elimination of All Forms of Racial Discrimination (21 December 1965)
International Convention on the Suppression and Punishment of the Crime of Apartheid (30 November 1973)
Declaration on Race and Racial Prejudice (27 November 1978)
Declaration on Fundamental Principles concerning the Contribution to the Mass Media to Strengthening Peace and International Understanding, to the Promotion of Human Rights and to Countering Racialism, Apartheid and Incitement to War (28 November 1978)
International Convention against Apartheid in Sports (10 December 1985)
Declaration on the Elimination of All Forms of Intolerance and of Discrimination based on Religion or Belief (25 November 1981)
Declaration on the Rights of Persons Belonging to National or Ethnic, Religious and Linguistic Minorities (18 December 1992)

Rights of women
Convention on the Political Rights of Women (20 December 1952, in effect 7 July 1957)
Declaration on the Protection of Women and Children in Emergency and Armed Conflict (14 December 1974)
Declaration on the Elimination of All Forms of Discrimination against Women (7 November 1967, into effect 3 September 1981)
Convention on the Elimination of All Forms of Discrimination against Women (20 November 1989)
Declaration on the Elimination of Violence against Women (20 December 1993)

Optional Protocol to the Convention on the Elimination of Discrimination against Women (10 December 1999, into effect 22 December 2000)

Rights of the child
Declaration on the Rights of the Child (20 November 1959)
Declaration on Social and Legal Principles relating to the Protection and Welfare of Children, with Special Reference to Foster Placement and Adoption Nationally and Internationally (3 December 1986)
Convention on the Rights of the Child (20 November 1989, into effect 2 September 1990)
Optional protocol to the Convention on the Rights of the Child on the involvement of children in armed conflict (25 May 2000, into effect 12 February 2002)
Optional protocol to the Convention on the Rights of the Child on the sale of children, child prostitution and child pornography (25 May 2000, into effect 18 January 2002)

Slavery, servitude, forced labour and similar institutions and practices
Slavery Convention (25 September 1926, into effect 9 March 1927)
Forced Labour Convention (28 June 1930, into effect 1 May 1932)
Convention for the Suppression of the Traffic in Persons and of the Exploitation of the Prostitution of Others (2 December 1949, into effect 25 July 1951)
Protocol amending the Slavery Convention (23 October 1953, into effect 7 December 1953)
Supplementary Convention on the Abolition of Slavery, the Slave Trade, and Institutions and Practices Similar to Slavery (30 April 1956/7 September 1956, into effect 30 April 1957)
Abolition of Forced Labour Convention (25 June 1957, into effect 17 January 1959)

Human rights in the administration of justice
Standard Minimum Rules for the Treatment of Prisoners (1955; 31 July 1957; 13 May 1977)
Code of Conduct for Law Enforcement Officials (17 December 1979)
Principles of Medical Ethics relevant to the Role of Health Personnel, particularly Physicians, in the Protection of Prisoners and Detainees against Torture and Other Cruel, Inhuman or Degrading Treatment or Punishment (18 December 1982)
Safeguards guaranteeing protection of the rights of those facing the death penalty (25 May 1984)
Basic Principles on the Independence of the Judiciary (26 August – 6 September 1985/29 November 1985/13 December 1985)
Declaration on the Protection of All Persons from Being Subjected to Torture and Other Cruel, Inhuman or Degrading Treatment or Punishment (10 December 1984, into effect 26 June 1987)
Body of Principles for the Protection of All Persons under Any Form of Detention or Imprisonment (9 December 1988)
Principles on the Effective Prevention and Investigation of Extra-legal, Arbitrary and Summary Executions (29 May 1989)
Declaration of Basic Principles of Justice for Victims of Crime and Abuse of Power (29 November 1985)

United Nations Standard Minimum Rules for the Administration of Juvenile Justice ('The Beijing Rules') (29 November 1989)

Basic Principles on the Use of Force and Firearms by Law Enforcement Officials (27 August– 7 October 1990)

Basic Principles on the Role of Lawyers (27 August – 7 October 1990)

Guidelines on the Role of Prosecutors (27 August – 7 October 1990)

United Nations Standard Minimum Rules for Non-custodial Measures ('The Tokyo Rules') (10 December 1990)

United Nations Rules for the Protection of Juveniles Deprived of the Liberty (14 December 1990)

Basic Principles for the Treatment of Prisoners (14 December 1990)

United Nations Guidelines for the Prevention of Juvenile Delinquency (The Riyadh Guidelines) (14 December 1990)

Model Treaty on the Transfer of Proceedings in Criminal Matters (14 December 1990)

Model Treaty on the Transfer of Supervision of Offenders Conditionally Sentenced or Conditionally Released (14 December 1990)

Declaration on the Protection of All Persons from Enforced Disappearances (18 December 1992)

Principles on the Effective Investigation and Documentation of Torture and Other Cruel, Inhuman or Degrading Treatment or Punishment (2 December 2000)

Convention against Torture and Other Cruel, Inhuman or Degrading Treatment or Punishment (4 December 2000)

Freedom of information

Convention on the International Right of Correction (16 December 1952, into effect 24 August 1962)

Freedom of association

Freedom of Association and Protection of the Right to Organise Convention (9 July 1948, into effect 4 July 1950)

Right to Organise and Collective Bargaining Convention (1 July 1949, into effect 18 July 1951)

Workers' Representatives Convention (23 June 1973, into effect 30 June 1973)

Labour Relations (Public Service) Convention (27 June 1978, into effect 25 February 1981)

Employment

Convention (No. 154) concerning the Promotion of Collective Bargaining (19 July 1981, into effect 11 August 1951)

Employment Policy Convention (9 July 1964, into effect 15 July 1966)

Convention (No. 168) concerning Employment Promotion and Protection against Unemployment (21 June 1988, into effect 17 October 1991)

Convention (No. 169) concerning Indigenous and Tribal Peoples in Independent Countries (21 June 1989, into effect 5 September 1991)

Marriage, Family and Youth

Convention on Consent to Marriage, Minimum Age for Marriage and Registration of Marriages (7 November 1962, into effect 9 December 1964)

Recommendation on Consent to Marriage, Minimum Age for Marriage and Registration of Marriages (1 November 1965)

Declaration on the Promotion among Youth of the Ideals of Peace, Mutual Respect and Understanding between Peoples (7 December 1965)

Social welfare, progress and development

Universal Declaration on the Eradication of Hunger and Malnutrition (16 November 1964)

Declaration on Social Progress and Development (11 December 1969)

Declaration on the Rights of Mentally Retarded Persons (20 December 1971)

Declaration on the Use of Scientific and Technological Progress in the Interests of Peace and for the Benefit of Mankind (10 November 1975)

Declaration on the Rights of Disabled Persons (9 December 1975)

Declaration on the Right of Peoples to Peace (12 November 1984)

Declaration on the Right to Development (4 December 1986)

Guidelines for the Regulation of Computerized Personal Data Files (14 December 1990)

International Convention on the Protection of the Rights of All Migrant Workers and Members of Their Families (18 December 1990)

Principles for the protection of persons with mental illness and the improvement of mental health care (17 December 1991)

Universal Declaration on the Human Genome and Human Rights (UNESCO) (2001)

Right to enjoy culture, international cultural development and co-operation

Declaration of the Principles of International Cultural Co-operation (UNESCO) (4 November 1966)

Recommendation concerning Education for International Understanding, Co-operation and Peace and Education relating to Human Rights and Fundamental Freedoms (UNESCO) (19 November 1974)

Nationality, statelessness, asylum and refugees

Statute of the Office of the United Nations High Commissioner for Refugees (14 December 1950)

Convention relating to the Status of Refugees (28 July 1951, into effect 22 April 1954)

Convention relating to the Status of Stateless Persons (28 September 1954, into effect 6 June 1960)

Convention on the Nationality of Married Women (29 January 1957, into effect 11 August 1958)

Protocol relating to the Status of Refugees (18 November 1966, into effect 4 October 1967)

Declaration on Territorial Asylum (14 December 1967)

Convention on the Reduction of Statelessness (30 August 1961, into effect 13 December 1975)

Declaration on the Human Rights of Individuals Who are not Nationals of the Country in which They Live (13 December 1985)

War crimes and crimes against humanity, including genocide
Convention on the Prevention and Punishment of the Crime of Genocide (9 December 1948, into effect 12 January 1951)
Convention on the Non-Applicability of Statutory Limitations to War Crimes and Crimes against Humanity (29 November 1968, into effect 11 November 1970)
Principles of international co-operation in the detection, arrest, extradition and punishment of persons guilty of war crimes and crimes against humanity (3 December 1973)

Humanitarian law
Geneva Convention for the Amelioration of the Condition of the Wounded and Sick in Armed Forces in the Field (21 April–12 August 1949, into effect 21 October 1950)
Geneva Convention for the Amelioration of the Condition of Wounded, Sick and Shipwrecked Members of Armed Forces at Sea (21 April–12 August 1949, into effect 21 October 1950)
Geneva Convention relative to the Treatment of Prisoners of War (21 April–12 August 1949, into effect 21 October 1950)
Geneva Convention relative to the Protection of Civilian Persons in Time of War (21 April–12 August 1949, into effect 21 October 1950)
Protocol Additional to the Geneva Conventions of 12 August 1949, and relating to the Protection of Victims of International Armed Conflicts (Protocol I) (8 June 1977, into effect 1979)
Protocol Additional to the Geneva Conventions of 12 August 1949, and relating to the Protection of Victims of Non-International Armed Conflicts (Protocol II) (8 June 1977, into effect 1979)

Appendix 2

Useful websites linked to key themes in citizenship and human rights education

Legal and human rights

Amnesty International	**www.ai.org.uk**
Anti-Slavery International	**www.antislavery.org**
Centre for Research in Human Rights	**www.roehampton.ac.uk**
Charter 88	**www.charter88.org.uk**
Citizen 21	**www.citizen21.org.uk**
Human Rights Watch	**www.hrw.org**
International PEN (Poets, Essayists, Novelists)	**www.pen.org.uk**
Survival	**www.survival-international.org**
The Hansard Society	**www.hansardsociety.org.uk**
United Nations	**www.un.org**

Diversity of national, regional, religious and ethnic identities in the UK

Buddhism	**www.buddhistnet.co.uk**
	www.dharmanet.org
	www.fwbo.org
	www.home.earthlink.org
	www.zen-izauk.org
Christian Education	**www.ce.org.uk**
Clear Vision (Buddhism)	**www.clear-vision.org.uk**
Channel 4 Black and Asian History Map	**www.channel4.com/blackhistorymap**
Commission for Racial Equality	**www.cre.gov.uk**
Crosspoint Anti-Racism	**www.magenta.nl/crosspoint**

English Heritage	www.english-heritage.org.uk
Hinduism	www.swaminarayan
Institute of Race Relations	www.irr.org.uk
Islam	www.muslimdirectory.co.uk
Judaism	www.jewish.co.uk
National Assembly for Wales	www.wales.gov.uk
Northern Ireland Assembly	www.ni-assembly.gov.uk
Operation Black Vote	www.obv.org.uk
Scottish Parliament	www.scottishparliament.uk
Sikhism	www.sikh.org
	www.sikhnet.org
The National Society (Church of England)	www.natsoc.org.uk
The National Trust	www.nationaltrsut.org.uk

Parliament, government and the courts

10 Downing Street	www.pm.gov.uk
British Monarchy	www.royal.gov.uk
Citizens Connection	www.citizenscnnection.net
CommonLink	www.montageplus.co.uk/commonlink
Explore Parliament	www.explore.parliament.uk
Home Office	www.homeoffice.gov.uk
Locata MP	www.locata.co.uk/commons
UK Online	www.ukonline.gov.uk
Y Vote	www.learn.co.uk/yvote
YouGov.com	www.yougov.com
Young People's Parliament	www.ypp.org.uk
YourTurn.net	www.yourturn.net

The media

Amazon	www.amazon.co.uk
BBC News Online	www.bbc.co.uk
BBC	www.bbc.co.uk/schools
Channel 4	www.4learning.co.uk

ITV	**www.itv.co.uk**
The Guardian	**www.guardian.co.uk**
Hodder and Stoughton	**www.educational-hodder.co.uk**
Heinemann	**www.heinemann.co.uk**
Nelson Thornes	**www.nelsonthornes.com**
RoutledgeFalmer	**www.routledgefalmer.com**
The Times Educational Supplement	**www.tes.co.uk**
Trentham Books	**www.trentham-books.co.uk**

The economy

British Council	**www.britishcouncil.org**
Consumer Gateway	**www.consumer.gov.uk**
Department of Trade and Industry Enterprise Guide	**www.dti.gov.uk**
Ofthelp	**www.ofthelp.com**
Personal Finance Education Group	**www.pfeg.org.uk**
Tourism Concern	**www.tourismconcern.org.uk**
Trading Standards	**www.tradingstandards.gov.uk**
Watchdog	**www.bbc.co.uk/watchdog**
Institute for Public Policy Research	**www.ippr.org.uk**

UK relations within Europe, the Commonwealth and the United Nations

Council of Europe – Education	**www.coe.fr/edu/eng**
Erasmus Student Network	**www.esn.org**
European Schoolnet	**www.eun.org**
European Union	**www.europa.org**
European Union	**www.europa.eu.int**
Imperial War Museum	**www.iwm.org.uk**
Commonwealth Secretariat	**www.thecommonwealth.org**
United Nations	**www.un.org**

Global interdependence and responsibility including sustainable development

Centre for Global and DevelopmentEducation	www.glade.org
Community Recycling Network	www.crn.org.uk
Cool Planet, Oxfam	www.oxfam.org.uk/coolplanet
Council for Environmental Education	www.cee.org.uk
Development Education Association	www.dea.gov.uk
Department for International Development	www.development.gov.uk
Education, The Environment Agency	www.environment-agency.gov.uk
Funergy	www.funergy.org.uk
Future Forests	www.futureforest.com
Global Dimension	www.globaldimension.org.uk
Global Gang	www.globalgang.org.uk
Greenpeace	www.greenpeace.org.uk
Learning Through Landscapes	www.ltl.org.uk
New Internationalist	www.newint.org
One World	www.oneworld.org
Planet Energy	www.dti.gov.uk/renewable
Regional Environmental Education Forum	www.schools.emnet.co.uk
Save the Children UK	www.savethechildren.co.uk
The Refugee Council	www.therefugeecouncil.org.uk
Tourism Concern	www.tourismconcern.org.uk
UN High Commissioner for Refugees	www.unhcr.org
UNICEF UK	www.unicef.org.uk
World Wildlife Fund UK	www.wwflearning.co.uk

Opportunities for effecting change

British Sports Trust	www.thebritishsportstrust.org.uk
British Youth Council	www.byc.org.uk

Citizens Connection	**www.citizensconnection.net**
Community Recycling Network	**www.crn.org.uk**
CSV Community Partners	**www.csv.co.uk**
Duke of Edinburgh's Award	**www.theaward.org**

Education Extra/Diana Princess of Wales

Memorial Award for Young People	**www.educationextra.org.uk**
Moral Courage Awards	**www.annefrank.org.uk**
National Youth Agency	**www.nya.org.uk**
Philip Lawrence Awards	**www.homeoffice.gov.uk/lawrence**
Schools Councils UK	**www.schoolscouncil.org**
The Prince's Trust	**www.princes-trust.org.uk**
Weston Spirit	**www.westonspirit.org.uk**
World Wildlife Fund UK	**www.wwflearning.co.uk**
YouthOrg	**www.youth.org.uk**